Divine Dialogue

Christian Responses to Modern-Day Skepticism

by
Yesu Vi

To you,

Stay Blessed

Table of Contents

Introduction:
Embracing the Conversation - Understanding Modern-Day Skepticism and Christian Apologetics

In an era where skepticism seems to burgeon with each passing day, the art of conversation, especially on matters of faith and belief, has never been more critical. The journey into understanding modern-day skepticism alongside Christian apologetics is not merely an academic exercise but a deep, soulful exploration into the very essence of what we hold to be true.

At the heart of these discussions lies a profound yearning for understanding, a quest for truth that transcends the mere accumulation of knowledge. It's about embarking on a path that could transform the way we perceive the world and our place within it. For Christians seeking to deepen their understanding of their faith, and for the curious minds exploring Christian perspectives, this journey is not only about defending beliefs but about opening doors to thoughtful engagement with skepticism and seekers alike.

The landscape of modern skepticism is vast and varied. It encompasses a wide array of doubts, from questioning the historical existence of Jesus to the role of miracles in the contemporary world. Skepticism challenges us to look deeper, to analyze our beliefs, and to articulate our faith with greater clarity and confidence. It compels us to engage in conversations that matter, conversations that bridge divides and foster understanding.

Christian apologetics, in this context, serves as a beacon of light. It offers a framework through which we can navigate the often turbulent waters of doubt and disbelief. It equips us with the tools to counter challenges with grace and to present reasoned, intellectually robust responses to the questions posed by skeptics. Apologetics does not seek to merely win arguments but to illuminate minds and touch hearts.

The goal of this exploration is not to provide simple answers to complex questions. Rather, it's about cultivating a spirit of inquiry, a willingness to delve into the depths of both skepticism and faith to uncover the nuances and intricacies that define them. It's about fostering a dialogue that respects differing viewpoints while standing firm in one's own convictions.

Embracing this conversation requires courage. It demands an openness to question and be questioned, to listen earnestly, and to engage respectfully. It is in the crucible of dialogue that the strength of our beliefs is tested and the beauty of genuine understanding can emerge.

As we venture into this exploration, let's do so with humility and confidence. Humility, in recognizing that we do not have all the answers, and confidence, in the resilience and relevance of the Christian faith. This journey is about more than defending a set of beliefs; it's about engaging with the world in a way that reflects the transformative power of faith.

This introduction sets the stage for a deeper dive into the core topics that shape the dialogue between skepticism and Christian apologetics. From the historical underpinnings of Jesus' existence to the philosophical discussions surrounding miracles, faith, and reason, we shall traverse a rich landscape of thought and belief.

As we explore the perplexing issue of evil and suffering, the conversation will extend into understanding the intersection of Christianity with other religions, the reliability of scripture, and the central tenet of the resurrection. We will delve into contemporary debates on morality, ethics, creation, and evolution, illuminating the Christian perspective on each.

The power of personal testimony and the role of Christians in public discourse will also be explored, offering insights into how apologetics can be lived out daily. This journey is not just about acquiring knowledge but about profoundly transforming how we engage with our faith and the world around us.

Let this exploration be a call to informed faith. A call to embrace the conversation with open hearts and minds, to seek truth with relentless curiosity, and to engage with the world with a spirit of love and understanding. May we be inspired to equip ourselves not only with answers but with questions that invite dialogue, encourage exploration, and foster genuine connections.

In embracing this conversation, we acknowledge that the dialogue between skepticism and faith is not a battleground but a fertile ground for growth. It's an opportunity to witness the power of Christian apologetics in bridging gaps, illuminating minds, and touching hearts.

As we move forward, let us hold onto the promise that in seeking, we shall find; in questioning, we shall uncover deeper truths; and in conversing, we shall foster understanding that transcends boundaries. This is the heart of apologetics - a journey not just toward defending our faith but toward living it out authentically and passionately in a skeptical world.

So, let us embark on this journey together, embracing the conversation with eagerness and hope. Let us explore, question, and engage, for it is in the richness of this dialogue that our faith can shine brightest.

Chapter 1:
The Historical Jesus - Separating
Fact from Fiction

In our journey to deepen understanding and engage thoughtfully with questions surrounding our faith, we embark on an examination of one of Christianity's most pivotal figures - Jesus of Nazareth. It's a quest that challenges us to sift through the sands of history, separating the bedrock of fact from the sediments of fiction. This chapter seeks to illuminate the historical Jesus, an endeavor that necessitates a diligent scrutiny of evidence and a keen understanding of historical methodology. By stepping outside the familiar realm of the Bible and exploring sources and traditions external to sacred scripture, we gain a broader perspective on the life and times of Jesus. This is not to dilute the scriptural narrative but to enrich our comprehension of it in the light of historical scrutiny. Addressing claims that reduce the figure of Jesus to myth, we venture into a rigorous analysis, bolstered by scholarly research and archaeological findings, to present a compelling case for the historical existence of Jesus. Our aim is not merely to affirm our faith but to equip every reader with an intellectual foundation, enabling confident discussions about Jesus's life and legacy in the modern world. Here, at the confluence of faith and reason, we invite you to rediscover Jesus, balanced at the crossroads of historical fact and heartfelt conviction.

The Quest for the Historical Jesus

In embarking on the quest for the historical Jesus, we confront a journey that compels us to sift through the sands of time, to discern truth amidst the echoes of centuries past. This venture is not merely an academic exercise; it is a heartfelt pursuit that calls upon us to engage deeply with history, culture, and spirituality. Our mission is to traverse beyond the familiar bounds of the Biblical texts, venturing into the realm of historical analysis and archaeological evidence, to construct a portrait of Jesus that resonates with authenticity and profound historical insight. By employing the rigorous tools of the historical method, we seek to illuminate the life and teachings of Jesus in a manner that both enlightens and inspires. This path invites us to confront our perceptions, challenge our understandings, and enrich our faith with a deeper comprehension of the historical figure at the heart of Christianity. As we navigate this journey, let us remain open to the transformative power of discovery, allowing our quest for the historical Jesus to not only inform our intellects but to kindle a more profound and invigorated expression of faith.

Sources Beyond the Bible

In departing from our exploration of the life and historical significance of Jesus, we transition into a realm equally fascinating: evidence outside the biblical narrative. This journey into sources beyond the Bible represents a bridge connecting faith with the broader context of history. It's not just a quest for corroborating evidence; it's an invitation to see the imprints of a spiritual journey documented across various cultures and epochs.

The importance of these external sources cannot be overstressed. They provide an invaluable perspective that enriches our understanding of the early Christian era and the figure of Jesus himself. Historians and scholars across centuries have leaned on these materials to construct a more detailed tapestry of the past. It's akin to discovering new hues and shades that enable a painting to come alive with depth and vibrancy.

Among these sources, works of Roman historians like Tacitus and Jewish historians like Josephus are particularly noteworthy. Tacitus, in his Annals, mentions "Christus," from whom the name "Christian" had its origins. This reference not only confirms the historical existence of Jesus but also touches upon the persecution of Christians in Rome. Josephus' works, specially "Antiquities of the Jews," offer accounts of Jesus that align with the biblical narrative, affirming his existence and execution.

These accounts, though limited in detail, are critical in establishing the historical presence of Jesus outside the biblical texts. Their value lies not just in historical validation but in the rich cultural contexts they provide, offering insights into the complexities of the times in which Jesus lived. These glimpses into Roman and Jewish perspectives highlight the profound impact Jesus had on various societies and classes.

Furthermore, archaeological discoveries also contribute to our understanding. From inscriptions and ancient manuscripts to artifacts and architectural ruins, each discovery adds a layer of knowledge about the societal, political, and religious dynamics of the ancient world. These findings help us grasp the physical reality of the world that Jesus inhabited and the early Christian community.

Gnostic texts, such as those found in Nag Hammadi, also offer a divergent look at early Christian thought and the figure of Jesus. Although these texts are not considered canonical, they are invaluable in understanding the diversity of early Christian beliefs and the development of Christian doctrine. It's essential to approach these texts not as conflicting voices but as part of the broader conversation about the spiritual and historical landscape of the time.

Another significant set of sources includes the writings of early Church Fathers, such as Clement of Rome, Ignatius of Antioch, and Justin Martyr. Their letters and scholarly works provide a direct link to the teachings and beliefs of early Christians. Through their writings, we can trace the development of early Christian communities, their struggles, and their faith.

Engaging with these sources invites us into a multifaceted dialogue that spans beyond the purely religious. It's a dialogue that encompasses history, culture, philosophy, and theology. This engagement isn't merely an academic exercise; it's a journey toward understanding our spiritual heritage and the foundational truths of Christianity in a broader context.

It's critical, however, to approach these sources with discernment. Not all writings outside the biblical canon offer the same level of reliability or insight into Jesus' life and the early Christian community. The task of sifting through these sources, discerning their authenticity and relevance, is both challenging and rewarding. It requires a commitment to intellectual honesty and a willingness to encounter complexity and ambiguity.

The exploration of sources beyond the Bible ultimately serves to deepen our faith. It presents an opportunity to confront our beliefs with historical evidence, to question and to seek understanding, not to undermine faith but to solidify it. This journey of discovery enables us to engage more meaningfully with skeptics and seekers, offering reasoned and nuanced responses to their queries.

Moreover, this exploration enhances our appreciation for the divine narrative. It allows us to see how the story of Jesus and early Christianity intersects with broader historical narratives, affirming the universality and timelessness of the Christian message. It's a testament to how Christianity has shaped, and been shaped by, the human experience across millennia.

In sum, sources beyond the Bible enrich our perception of Christianity, grounding it in a historical context that is both profound and illuminating. They open up avenues for dialogue and understanding, inviting us to appreciate the depth and breadth of our faith. This path, paved with evidence and reason, leads us not away from faith, but deeper into it, affirming the historical foundation of our beliefs and inviting us to embrace our spiritual heritage with confidence and conviction.

As we continue to explore these sources, let us do so with open hearts and minds. Let the knowledge we gain fortify our faith, inspiring us to live out our beliefs with renewed passion and purpose. Let it remind us that our faith is not a relic of the past but a living, breathing testament to the enduring presence of the divine in the world. In this journey of discovery, let us find not just evidence of historical truth but a deeper connection to the spiritual lineage that binds us all.

Thus, the exploration of sources beyond the Bible not only enriches our understanding of Christianity but also reinforces the bridge between faith and reason. It's an invitation to view our spiritual journey within the vast expanse of human history and experience, and to recognize the profound ways in which the message of Christ transcends time and culture. Through this exploration, we can navigate the modern world with the wisdom of the past, equipped to face challenges and opportunities with grace, understanding, and a deeply rooted faith.

The Historical Method and Jesus

In undertaking the quest to understand the historical Jesus, it's paramount to employ the historical method with precision and rigor. This method, a cornerstone in the field of historical inquiry, enables us to sift through the layers of history to uncover facts and form a coherent narrative about figures and events of the past. When applied to the life and teachings of Jesus Christ, this method does not merely affirm faith; it illuminates the historical underpinnings of the Gospel narratives, offering a bridge between faith and historical evidence.

The historical method involves several key steps: critical analysis of sources, evaluation of the historical context, corroboration from multiple sources, and the distinction between primary and secondary sources. These steps form a framework through which the life of Jesus can be examined, not as a matter of mere belief, but as a subject of historical investigation.

When approaching the Gospels with the historical method, the first step is to scrutinize these texts with the same critical eye that historians use for any ancient documents. This involves questioning the authorship, date of writing, intended audience, and purposes behind the texts. Such an inquiry does not diminish the spiritual value of these writings; rather, it seeks to understand them within their historical context, enhancing our appreciation of their message.

Furthermore, the historical method leads us to explore sources beyond the Bible that reference Jesus. These include writings by Josephus, Tacitus, and Pliny the Younger, among others. While these sources are not without their own biases and limitations, their accounts provide corroborative evidence that Jesus was a historical figure, known beyond the early Christian communities.

Corroboration plays a crucial role in the historical method. By considering the Gospel accounts alongside external sources, historians can identify core elements of Jesus's life that are widely attested. This convergence of evidence strengthens the historical case for Jesus's existence and his impact on the first-century world.

Understanding the historical Jesus also requires an appreciation for the sociopolitical context of first-century Judea. The Roman occupation, Jewish religious expectations of a Messiah, and the diverse sects within Judaism all influenced the reception of Jesus's message. The historical method allows us to tease out these layers, portraying Jesus as a figure who both emerged from and profoundly challenged his historical setting.

The distinction between primary and secondary sources is another key element of the historical method. The New Testament writings, especially the Pauline epistles and the Synoptic Gospels, are considered primary sources for the study of Jesus. They bear witness to the beliefs and experiences of the earliest Christian communities. Secondary sources, including the writings of early church fathers and later historians, provide additional perspectives but are evaluated for their proximity to the events they describe.

Applying the historical method to Jesus's teachings reveals themes and ideas that resonated within first-century Judaism while also pointing beyond it. Parables, ethical teachings, prophetic pronouncements, and claims of divine authority are examined not just as religious texts but as historical artifacts that shed light on Jesus's person and mission.

Such an examination does not reduce the figure of Jesus to a mere historical curiosity. On the contrary, it challenges us to consider the implications of his life and teachings in their historical context. How did a Jewish preacher from Galilee inspire a movement that would grow to become a world religion? What can the historical method tell us about the claims of his divinity and resurrection? These are not questions that push faith to the sidelines; rather, they invite a deeper engagement with faith through the lens of history.

It's essential to acknowledge the limits of the historical method. While it can provide insights into the life of Jesus, it operates within the realm of probability rather than certainty. Historical inquiry can point us toward the most reasonable conclusions based on available evidence, but it does not offer the final word on matters of faith. The historical Jesus, as reconstructed through scholarly methods, provides a compelling portrait, yet it is ultimately incomplete without the lens of faith.

This recognition leads us to a profound intersection of faith and history. Believers are called not to abandon reason in the pursuit of faith but to engage it fully, exploring the historical foundations of Christianity with an open heart and mind. This journey does not weaken faith; it enriches it, grounding belief in the soil of history and human experience.

Therefore, let us approach the quest for the historical Jesus not as a challenge to faith but as an opportunity to deepen it. Let us use the historical method not as a tool to dissect our beliefs but as a means to understand them more fully. In doing so, we honor the God who invites us to love Him with all our mind, as well as our heart and soul.

Engaging with the historical Jesus also empowers Christians to participate in informed discussions about their faith. In a world where skepticism often challenges religious beliefs, understanding the historical evidence for Jesus's life and teachings equips believers to respond thoughtfully. It fosters a faith that is not only heartfelt but also intellectually robust and defensible.

In conclusion, the journey into the historical method and Jesus is a transformative one. It beckons us to merge the paths of faith and reason, leading to a deeper, more nuanced understanding of Christianity. Through this journey, our faith is not only affirmed but invigorated, enabling us to meet the challenges of the modern world with confidence and grace. Let this exploration be a testament to our unyielding quest for truth, guided by the spirit of inquiry and the light of faith.

Responding to Claims of Mythology

In navigating the landscape of modern skepticism, one of the most prevalent challenges faced by Christianity is the assertion that the narrative of Jesus Christ is rooted in mythology rather than historical fact. This chapter aims to address these claims head-on, equipping believers with the knowledge to respond confidently to such criticisms, and inspiring those on the fence to look deeper into the credibility of the Christian faith.

At the heart of the argument against the historical Jesus is the notion that stories of His life, miracles, and resurrection are too similar to mythological tales from other ancient cultures. Some suggest that Christianity merely borrowed extensively from earlier myths, repackaging them into a new religious narrative. Here, it's crucial to differentiate between superficial similarities and substantive evidence.

First and foremost, the existence of Jesus Christ as a historical figure is well-documented, not only within the canonical texts of the Bible but also in the works of early non-Christian historians like Tacitus and Josephus. These accounts provide independent attestation of His life and the impact of His teachings, setting a foundation for addressing the mythology claim from a standpoint of historical credibility.

Furthermore, the historical method — when applied rigorously to the sources concerning Jesus — supports the reliability of the Gospel narratives. The criteria of embarrassment, multiple attestation, and coherence, among others, are used by historians to assess the likelihood of an event's historicity. Many key events in the life of Jesus, including His crucifixion, meet these criteria in ways that mythological stories do not.

It's also important to understand the context in which these stories were written. The Gospels were penned in a historical and cultural milieu vastly different from the mythological narratives of ancient Greece or Egypt, for example. The Gospel writers had a commitment to preserving the teachings and events they believed were not only true but foundational to the faith they practiced and sought to spread. This is a far cry from the creation of myths intended to explain natural phenomena or illustrate moral truths through allegory.

The claim that Christianity synthesized its teachings from prior myths fails to acknowledge the uniqueness of Jesus' life and message. Unlike mythical deities, Jesus lived in a specific historical and geographical context. His teachings, parables, and actions were deeply embedded in the sociopolitical realities of 1st-century Judea, addressing issues of poverty, social justice, and spiritual integrity in ways that were revolutionary for His time.

When discussing the miraculous aspects of Jesus' life, it's vital to approach the subject with an understanding that the worldview of ancient peoples included a belief in the supernatural. However, the intention behind the Gospel accounts was not to fabricate wonder-working capabilities for the sake of awe. Rather, the miracles of Jesus are presented as signs of His authority and divinity, fulfilling Old Testament prophecies and affirming His messages of love, forgiveness, and redemption.

The resurrection of Jesus, arguably the most contested aspect of His story, is supported by a wealth of historical evidence and eyewitness testimony, as documented within the New Testament texts and corroborated by early Christian writers. The transformation of His followers, willing to face persecution and death for their unwavering belief in His resurrection, speaks volumes to the authenticity and impact of this event.

In responding to claims of mythology, it's also beneficial to point out the transformative power of Christianity throughout history. The teachings of Jesus have permeated cultures worldwide, inspiring movements for social justice, human rights, and compassion that reflect the profound truth and moral depth of His message.

Encountering skepticism with grace and informed dialogue opens opportunities for meaningful conversation about faith, doubt, and the search for truth. It's through these discussions that the beauty and historical grounding of Christianity can shine, touching hearts and minds in a world yearning for genuine connection and understanding.

To those questioning the historicity of Jesus and the veracity of the Christian faith, we invite you to look beyond surface comparisons with mythology. Explore the historical evidence, engage with the scholarly research, and consider the personal testimonies of countless individuals transformed by an encounter with the risen Christ. In these pursuits, the truth of Christianity emerges not as a myth, but as a compelling narrative grounded in historical reality and alive with the promise of hope, love, and redemption.

As we wrap up this section, let's hold onto the conviction that our faith is built upon a foundation that withstands the scrutiny of history and criticism. Let's continue to engage with skeptics not as adversaries but as fellow seekers of truth, with the knowledge that it is in the depth of historical Jesus that the power and essence of Christianity truly unfold.

In conclusion, embracing the challenges posed by claims of mythology not only strengthens our faith but also enriches our understanding of the historical Jesus. By responding with fact-based evidence, reasoned arguments, and a spirit of open dialogue, we uphold the integrity of our beliefs and inspire others to explore the profound depths of Christianity. Let us move forward with confidence, knowing that the truth of Jesus Christ stands robust amidst the waves of skepticism, guiding us toward a deeper, more authentic faith.

Chapter 2:
Miracles and Mystery - Rationalizing the Supernatural

In our quest for understanding, Chapter 2 delves into the realm of miracles and mystery, addressing how these elements can be rationalized within a framework that often demands empirical evidence. To skeptics and believers alike, the concept of miracles represents a cornerstone of contention and fascination. This chapter aims to explore miracles not as anomalies defying logic, but as events inviting us to expand our understanding of the natural world. We'll examine how defining miracles in the context of a scientific age does not diminish their wonder but rather highlights the potential for harmony between faith and reason. Engaging with the philosophical arguments surrounding the possibility of miracles, we confront head-on the critiques posited by thinkers such as Hume, proposing counterarguments that reaffirm the coexistence of miracles and natural law. By integrating a reasoned approach to the supernatural, this exploration does not seek to explain away the mystery but to invite a deeper appreciation for the breadth and depth of divine engagement with the world. Through this journey, we aim to equip readers with a balanced perspective, empowering them to navigate discussions about the intersection of faith, miracles, and rational thought with confidence and a renewed sense of awe.

Defining Miracles in a Scientific Age

Within the heart of every believer and seeker lies a deep-seated quest for understanding the divine interventions that pepper our world's history - miracles. In this age of science and technology, defining miracles poses both a challenge and an opportunity for enriching our faith and broadening our perspective. It's essential to approach this exploration with an open heart and a mind willing to find harmony between the wonders of faith and the laws of nature.

To embark on this journey, we must first establish a clear definition of what constitutes a miracle. Traditionally, miracles have been viewed as events or occurrences that defy natural explanations, acts of divine intervention that signal the presence of a higher power at work. However, in a society that often seeks evidence-based explanations for the world around us, the traditional understanding of miracles invites scrutiny and skepticism.

Yet, it's crucial to recognize that the realm of the miraculous is not at odds with the world of science. Rather, miracles can be seen as extraordinary events that invite us to explore the depths of both faith and reason. They are not so much violations of natural laws, but as indications that the universe is underpinned by a wisdom and a power that transcend our understanding.

In redefining miracles for the modern age, we acknowledge that our scientific knowledge is ever-growing and evolving. What once seemed miraculous, seamlessly fitting into the category of the unexplainable, may now be understood through the lens of advanced scientific inquiry. This does not diminish the presence or the power of miracles; it simply calls us to adopt a more nuanced perspective.

Consider the intricacies of the human body, the complexity of our DNA, and the breathtaking beauty of the universe. These may not be miracles in the traditional sense - water turning into wine, the blind seeing, or the dead rising - but they speak to a miraculous reality nonetheless. The extraordinary complexity and order of the natural world can evoke a sense of wonder and awe that parallels the reactions evoked by traditional miracles.

This understanding urges us to see miracles not as exceptions to the natural order, but as profound manifestations of the divine within that order. It's a call to perceive the world around us, science and all, through a lens of wonder, recognizing divine fingerprints in the grand and the minute, the spectacular and the everyday.

For Christians navigating the waters of faith in a scientific age, embracing this expanded notion of miracles equips us to engage in meaningful dialogues with skeptics and seekers alike. It allows us to affirm the value of scientific inquiry while maintaining that the essence of the divine flows through and transcends it.

At the heart of acknowledging miracles in today's world is the understanding that faith and science are not competitors vying for the throne of truth but allies in the quest to understand the vastness of our universe and the one who created it. This perspective opens up a space for dialogue and exploration, where questions are welcomed and the mystery of faith is embraced rather than shunned.

It's vital, then, for believers to cultivate an openness to learning and a humility in the face of the unknown. The pursuit of understanding miracles in our age should not lead us to a rigid defense of our preconceptions but to a dynamic and ever-evolving faith that seeks understanding through the tools given to us by both revelation and reason.

Faced with the miraculous, be it in the guise of an inexplicable healing or the indescribable beauty of a starlit sky, our response as people of faith should be one of awe, gratitude, and a renewed commitment to explore the boundless depths of God's creation. The divine hand at work in the world invites us to wonder, to inquire, and to respond with lived faith that bears witness to the miraculous in our midst.

As we navigate this scientific era, let's encourage one another to broaden our horizons, to view miracles not as challenges to our intellect but as invitations to delve deeper into the mystery that is faith. In doing so, we build bridges between the world of science and the heart of faith, discovering along the way that miracles, in their essence, are a profound testament to a reality that is both seen and unseen, comprehensible and beyond our wildest comprehension.

Thus, in defining miracles in a scientific age, we come to a place of greater understanding and harmony between faith and reason. This journey does not weaken our faith; it strengthens it, offering us a richer, more vibrant, and more resilient belief system that can stand firm in the face of questions and doubts. It equips us to engage with the world in a manner that is both intellectually sound and spiritually nourishing.

Let us embrace this journey with open hearts and minds, eager to discover how the language of science and the language of faith can coalesce into a deeper, more fulfilling understanding of the divine. In this endeavor, we do not merely redefine miracles; we reclaim them, recognizing their power to transform hearts, minds, and souls in a scientific age.

By embracing miracles in this expanded, nuanced way, we invite both believers and skeptics to join us in a shared exploration of the wonderous complexity of our world. Together, let's discover the miraculous, not as a stumbling block to belief but as a stepping stone towards a greater, more comprehensive appreciation of the mystery that underpins our existence and beckons us towards the divine.

Philosophical Arguments for the Possibility of Miracles

In traversing the landscape where the palpable meets the profound, we encounter the stirring notion of miracles—a harbinger of hope that perplexes yet reassures. In the grand design where natural laws reign supreme, miracles appear as the divine brushstrokes that transcend human logic and understanding. Yet, it is through the lens of philosophy that we find a sanctuary for reason and belief to coalesce, offering a robust defense for the plausibility of miracles. Philosophers across ages have untangled this intricate dance between the possible and the extraordinary, suggesting that the very structure of reality is not opposed to occurrences beyond our normal experiences. They argue that if the cosmos is underpinned by a rational order, then it is conceivable for that order to have exceptions, should they serve a greater purpose. This is not to undermine the fabric of natural laws but to underline a profound flexibility in the cosmic order, orchestrated by a transcendent will. This philosophical stance does not frivolously accept miracles but invites a deeper exploration into the nature of reality, where the extraordinary is not dismissed but embraced as a testament to a greater narrative at play. It's in this exploration that believers find not just a defense for their faith, but a rejuvenating affirmation that at the heart of existence lies a mystery willing itself to be known, transforming skepticism into wonder and doubt into a journey of discovery.

Hume's Critique and Counterarguments

As we venture deeper into our exploration of the miraculous, it becomes essential to address a pivotal moment in the history of skepticism: David Hume's critique of miracles. Hume, an 18th-century philosopher, challenged the credibility of miraculous claims on the grounds that they are always based on insufficient evidence. He argued that a miracle, by definition, is a violation of the laws of nature. And since these laws are established by a firm and unalterable experience, the evidence supporting a miracle must be of such a kind that its falsehood would be more miraculous than the event it endeavors to establish.

Hume's argument has been a cornerstone for skeptics questioning the plausibility of miracles reported in religious texts, including Christianity. However, a thorough examination reveals that his critique, while influential, is not without its flaws. To engage meaningfully with those who find Hume's arguments compelling, one must first understand and then thoughtfully respond to these critiques.

At the heart of Hume's skepticism is an epistemological standard that privileges empirical evidence above all else. This stance, though valuable in many scientific inquiries, poses a significant limitation when applied to historical events or personal experiences. Miracles, by their very nature, do not conform to repeatable scientific experimentation. They are singular events that often serve a specific purpose at a particular moment in history. Therefore, dismissing their possibility a priori based on empirical standards alone narrows the scope of human understanding and inquiry.

Furthermore, Hume's insistence on the impossibility of miracles hinges on a circular argument. He presupposes that the laws of nature are immutable and universal, yet, the possibility of a divine intervention implies that these laws can be temporarily suspended by the Creator who established them. If one admits the existence of a Creator, the impossibility of miracles can't be asserted with the same certainty that Hume does.

Another critique of Hume's argument involves his assessment of human testimony. He assumes that people are prone to fallacy and exaggeration, especially in matters of religious significance. While it's true that not all testimonies are reliable, dismissing all miraculous claims based on this generalization overlooks the possibility of genuine, verifiable accounts. Not all witnesses are equally unreliable, and not all claims of miracles are equally implausible. The Christian tradition, for example, bases its claim of the resurrection of Jesus on multiple independent sources, a fact that demands a more nuanced approach than Hume's blanket skepticism.

Additionally, Hume fails to account for the cumulative case argument. This approach suggests that while any single piece of evidence for a miracle might not be compelling on its own, the convergence of multiple lines of evidence can provide a robust case for the miraculous. For Christianity, the historical reliability of the Gospel accounts, the transformation of the lives of the apostles, and the exponential growth of the early church under persecution serve as intersecting proofs that bolster the claim of Jesus's resurrection.

It's also essential to recognize that Hume's critique is based on a worldview that excludes the supernatural a priori. If one operates from a materialistic perspective, then miracles are, by definition, impossible. However, a worldview that allows for the existence of a Creator who interacts with creation opens the possibility for miracles. Philosophical naturalism cannot prove the non-existence of the supernatural; it can only assume it. Therefore, Hume's critique, far from being a neutral analysis, is deeply entrenched in a specific philosophical stance.

Another point to consider is the impact of miracles on faith. Hume seems to suggest that belief in miracles is founded on a fragile basis. However, from a Christian perspective, miracles are not merely arbitrary displays of power. They serve as signs pointing beyond themselves to deeper truths. The miracles of Jesus, for instance, reveal his compassion, his authority over creation, and his identity as the Son of God. They are not just violations of natural laws but manifestations of a deeper, divine reality.

In response to Hume, then, one must argue that his approach to evaluating miracles is constrained by an overly narrow epistemological framework and a philosophical commitment to naturalism. A more open-minded approach, one that allows for the possibility of a Creator and the potential for divine intervention, can find reasonable ground to consider miracles as historically plausible.

This does not mean that Christians should abandon critical thinking or skepticism towards miraculous claims. On the contrary, discernment is vital. Not every claim to the miraculous is genuine, and the Christian faith is not built on a blind acceptance of every supernatural claim. However, when approached with an open mind and heart, the testimonies of miracles, especially those foundational to Christian belief, offer a compelling case for the transcendent breaking into the immanent, inviting us into a deeper engagement with the mystery of faith.

In a world that yearns for certainty and empirical evidence, the challenge of Hume's critique can seem daunting. Yet, it's an opportunity for believers to delve deeper into the rationale of their faith, fortified by the knowledge that belief in miracles is not irrational. It's a stance that gracefully holds in tension the wonders of the natural world and the awe-inspiring possibility of the supernatural. In doing so, it beckons each of us to a journey that transcends the limits of empirical evidence, inviting us into a profound encounter with the divine.

Engaging with Hume's critique and its counterarguments is not an exercise in intellectual superiority or in discrediting the skeptic. It's an act of faith seeking understanding, an invitation to dialogue with open hearts and minds. Such engagement is fundamental to the Christian journey, which is marked by a relentless quest for truth, guided by the light of reason and the warmth of faith.

As we continue our exploration of the miraculous within Christianity, let us carry forward the courage to question, the humility to listen, and the wisdom to discern. The journey of faith is, after all, a pilgrimage of the heart, mind, and soul towards the fullness of truth. In this quest, the critique of Hume and the responses it elicits serve not as stumbling blocks but as stepping stones, enriching our understanding and deepening our faith.

Chapter 3:
Faith and Reason - Philosophy
in Christian Thought

As we delve into the rich tapestry of Christian philosophy, the intersection of faith and reason emerges as a crucial touchstone. The journey towards understanding Christianity doesn't ask us to leave reason at the door; rather, it invites a profound engagement with both heart and mind. Throughout history, Christian thought has been characterized not by a rejection of rational inquiry, but by a deep and compelling synthesis of faith with philosophical rigor. The harmony between faith and reason demands a nuanced appreciation, asserting that faith is not a blind leap into darkness but a well-lighted path walked with the guide of reason. This symbiosis is not a contradiction but a testament to the richness of Christian intellectual tradition, which holds that the truth about our world and our Creator is accessible both through the light of faith and the lens of critical thought. By exploring how faith can be reasonable, and how reason can lead to faith, this chapter addresses not only the skeptic's doubts but strengthens the believer's conviction, affirming that the pursuit of truth leads us closer to the divine, not farther from it.

The Reasonability of Faith

Faith is often perceived as a leap into the abyss of irrationality, a surrender of logic in favor of emotion. Yet, if we pause and explore the terrain of Christian thought with sincerity and an open heart, we find that faith is not a blind alley but a road that is accompanied by reason, a path that has been trodden by some of the most brilliant minds through the ages. This isn't about diminishing reason but about acknowledging that faith and reason can, and do, walk hand in hand.

Consider the universe, with its endless complexities and precise laws that govern the stars, planets, and the very atoms within our bodies. The belief in a Creator isn't a dismissal of science but a companion to it, encouraging us to seek and marvel at the intricacies of our world. This wonder doesn't contradict scientific inquiry; rather, it complements it, offering a perspective that sees beyond mere mechanics to purpose and intention.

In the history of Christian thought, numerous theologians and philosophers have demonstrated that faith is not at war with reason. Instead, they've shown that faith enriches our cognitive capacity, opening us to truths beyond the reach of empirical verification. Faith paves the way for a deeper understanding, one that encompasses both the seen and the unseen, the empirical and the metaphysical.

Moreover, the moral and ethical dimensions of our lives speak to the reasonability of faith. In a world where relativism often leaves us adrift, the moral compass provided by faith offers direction and clarity. This isn't about imposing a set of rules but about discovering a foundation for justice, love, and human dignity. Faith challenges us to look beyond our immediate desires and conveniences, urging us toward the greater good.

One might argue that belief in God is a psychological crutch, an invention to soothe our existential anxieties. Yet, if we dive deeper, isn't it also reasonable to consider that our desire for meaning, our appreciation for beauty, our quest for justice, and our yearning for love point toward something beyond ourselves? Isn't it plausible that these universal human experiences are indicators of a reality that transcends the material?

Christianity, at its core, isn't merely a set of doctrines but a relationship with a God who is both transcendent and immanent. Faith invites us into this relationship, not by sidelining our intellect but by engaging it along with our heart and soul. The Christian tradition is rich with practices and teachings that nourish both the mind and the spirit, fostering a faith that is both thoughtful and deeply felt.

Skeptics might question the relevance of faith in a modern, technological society. Yet, the enduring human questions about purpose, value, and meaning remain. Technology, for all its benefits, cannot answer these. Faith steps into this space, offering perspectives that enrich our understanding of ourselves, our place in the world, and our interactions with others.

Furthermore, the historical foundation of Christianity, underscored by the life, death, and resurrection of Jesus Christ, invites intellectual investigation. The claims of Christianity are not only spiritual but also historical, providing a tangible foothold for those who seek to explore faith with the tools of reason. The historical method itself has been applied to these claims, revealing a faith that welcomes scrutiny rather than shying away from it.

The testimonies of countless individuals throughout history add another layer to the reasonability of faith. From the early martyrs to contemporary believers, many have encountered Christianity not merely as a set of beliefs but as a transformative experience that stands up to both intellectual and existential inquiry. These testimonies serve as a living witness to the vibrancy and depth of faith.

It's crucial to remember that faith and reason each have their domain, their strengths, and their limitations. While reason helps us navigate the physical world and enhances our understanding through science and logic, faith accesses deeper existential truths, providing a broader context for our reasonings. Together, they form a more holistic apprehension of reality.

In approaching the relationship between faith and reason, it is beneficial to adopt a posture of humility. This humility acknowledges our finite understanding and opens us to the possibility of truths that surpass our current comprehension. It's in this humility that faith and reason can coexist, each enriching the other, guiding us toward a fuller understanding of truth.

At its heart, the Christian faith calls us not to a blind belief but to a reasoned trust. This trust is based on the historical person of Jesus Christ, the wonders of creation, the testimony of transformed lives, and the deep resonance of the Christian narrative with our most profound human experiences. It invites us into a relationship that engages all aspects of our being, offering a vision of life that is both intellectually satisfying and spiritually fulfilling.

As we navigate the complexities of the modern world, the reasonability of faith offers a beacon of hope. In a culture often marked by cynicism and disillusionment, faith opens us to a sense of wonder, purpose, and connection. It encourages us not only to ask the deep questions but also to live them, embodying the values of love, justice, and compassion in our daily lives.

In conclusion, embracing faith is not an abandonment of reason but a celebration of it. Faith expands the horizons of our understanding, inviting us into a deeper engagement with the world, with each other, and with the Divine. In this journey, faith and reason are not adversaries but allies, each playing a vital role in our quest for truth and meaning.

Compatibility of Faith with Science and Logic

In essence, the journey of faith is not one that necessitates the abandonment of logic or scientific understanding. Far from being at odds, faith and reason can coexist, intertwining seamlessly to enrich our comprehension of the universe and our place within it. This unity invites us to explore the vast expanse of human knowledge while rooted firmly in the spiritual conviction that informs our existence.

Central to the Christian tradition is the understanding that faith is not blind. It seeks understanding, as St. Anselm famously posited, "fides quaerens intellectum" - faith seeking understanding. This principle challenges us to engage deeply with our beliefs, scrutinizing them not as fragile constructs to be shielded from the harsh light of inquiry, but as truths robust enough to withstand rigorous examination.

The narrative that science and faith are perpetually at war is a modern myth, propagated by misunderstandings on both sides. From the onset, many pioneers of science were devout Christians, seeing their work as uncovering the ordered structure of God's creation. The meticulous order found in the cosmos, from the vast galaxies to the intricate design of DNA, echoes the majestic creativity of a Designer.

Logic, the bedrock of reasoned argument, plays a critical role in theology. Far from being a mere intellectual exercise, logical scrutiny within the Christian tradition serves to deepen our understanding of divine mysteries. The Trinity, the nature of Christ, and the concept of salvation have all been topics of meticulous logical exploration, demonstrating that faith seeks not to bypass reason but to surpass its bounds by embracing mysteries that logic alone cannot fully explain.

The discourse around miracles provides a fascinating intersection of faith, science, and logic. Miracles, by definition, are extraordinary events that defy natural explanations. Skeptics often cite miracles as a point of contention, arguing that they are incompatible with the laws of nature. However, if we conceive of God as the author of these laws, then surely the possibility of divine intervention remains within the realm of logical consistency. Miracles do not suspend the natural order; they manifest the freedom of its Creator to operate within His creation uniquely.

Historically, the Christian faith has contributed significantly to the development of scientific inquiry. The belief in a rational Creator encouraged the early Christian scholars to pursue studies of the natural world as a form of worship, revealing God's character and glory through His creation. This marriage of faith and science birthed breakthroughs in various fields, affirming that the pursuit of knowledge is a divine mandate.

Moreover, the complexity and beauty of the universe, as unveiled by science, can enhance our sense of wonder and lead us to reverence. From the microscopic to the macroscopic, every level of complexity reveals layers of order and design that can inspire a deeper appreciation for the Creator's ingenuity. The intricate details of living cells, the precise laws governing the cosmos, and the breathtaking beauty of nature all speak to a creative intellect behind the universe.

Reason and faith each have their own domains of authority and their own paths to knowledge. Faith encompasses the realms beyond the empirical, offering insights into questions of meaning, purpose, and value that science cannot adjudicate. Conversely, science provides a methodical approach to understanding the physical universe. Together, they form a comprehensive framework for understanding the multifaceted nature of reality.

Addressing the challenges posed by evolutionary theory, the Christian does not find a foe but an opportunity to marvel at the processes by which life diversifies and adapts. Rather than viewing evolution and creation as opposing theories, we can appreciate evolutionary science as a means of understanding the mechanisms God may use to unfold the diversity of life, revealing His omnipotence and wisdom in sustaining life's complexity and adaptability.

In engaging with both scientific discoveries and the mysteries of faith, a Christian perspective values humility. We acknowledge the limits of human understanding and the provisional nature of scientific theories, alongside the transcendent truths revealed through faith. This humility enables a posture of learning and openness, where questions and doubts are not feared but embraced as avenues of deeper exploration and understanding.

The logical coherence of the Christian worldview, rooted in the historical reality of the resurrection of Jesus, offers a compelling argument for the truth of Christianity. The resurrection, examined through the lens of historical evidence, fulfills criteria of historical reliability, providing a rational basis for faith that transcends mere philosophical speculation.

Philosophical debates around the existence of God, the problem of evil, and the nature of consciousness find their place within a framework of faith that respects logic and evidence. Christian apologetics engages these debates not with the aim of 'winning' arguments but with the intention of seeking truth, fostering understanding, and demonstrating the coherence and relevance of Christian belief in addressing the deepest human questions.

In practical terms, the integration of faith with science and logic equips believers to engage confidently in conversations about religion, philosophy, and science. Understanding that faith is not antithetical to reason enhances our ability to communicate effectively about the rational grounds for belief, inviting others into a thoughtful exploration of Christian faith.

Finally, the journey of faith enriched by science and reason is one of awe and wonder. It beckons us to look beyond the horizon of the material to the spiritual, beyond the known to the mystery, and beyond the temporal to the eternal. In seeking the unity of knowledge and faith, we find a holistic understanding that nourishes the mind, heart, and soul.

The pursuit of truth, in all its forms, is a noble endeavor that draws us closer to the Divine. As we explore the universe with open minds and hearts, may we find not only answers but also a deeper connection with the Creator, whose genius and love illuminate every aspect of our existence.

Chapter 4:
The Problem of Evil and Suffering - A Christian Perspective

In the heart of every person's quest for understanding lies the profound question of why evil and suffering exist. This chapter delves into the Christian perspective, which provides not only solace but also a compelling framework for grappling with this vexing issue. At the core of Christianity is the belief in a God who is both omnipotent and benevolently involved in the world. Yet, the existence of evil and suffering seems to challenge this notion on its face. However, when we explore the depths of Christian theology, we find that rather than evading this dilemma, it confronts it head-on. The concepts of free will and the fallen nature of the world are pivotal in this discourse. It's posited that God, in His infinite wisdom, granted humanity free will - a gift that carries with it the potential for misuse. It's within this misuse of free will that we find the genesis of much suffering and evil. But the narrative doesn't end there; it's further enriched by the doctrine of redemption and the promise of a world made anew. Thus, from a Christian standpoint, evil and suffering are not markers of a world abandoned by God but are instead pivotal elements within a larger cosmic story of love, freedom, and eventual restoration. This perspective invigorates believers to live with hope and to engage the suffering of the world not as passive spectators but as active agents of change, empowered by the promise of transformation and eternal peace.

Free Will and the Nature of God

In grappling with the complexities of evil and suffering, it's vital to explore the concepts of free will and the nature of God. These topics are not only central to understanding the Christian perspective on pain and misfortune but also offer profound insights into the depth of God's love and the value He places on our freedom.

At the heart of Christianity is the belief in a God who is both omnipotent and benevolent. This belief raises an immediate question: why would a loving and powerful God allow suffering to exist? The answer, which strikes at the core of this discussion, lies in the gift of free will bestowed upon humanity.

Free will, the ability to make choices without coercion, is a fundamental aspect of human experience. Its value cannot be overstated because it's what makes genuine love possible. Without free will, love would be programmed or forced, devoid of authenticity and meaning. Therefore, God, in His wisdom, chose to create beings with the capacity to choose love, fully knowing the risk involved—the potential for rejection and the emergence of evil.

This divinely granted freedom brings us to the doorstep of understanding why evil exists. Evil is not a creation of God, but rather the misuse of free will by humanity. When we choose actions that are contrary to goodness and love, we introduce suffering into the world. This is not a reflection of God's limitation or malevolence but a testament to the extent God respects our freedom to choose.

It's important to distinguish between two types of evil: moral evil, which results from human choices, and natural evil, such as natural disasters. While the former can be directly linked to free will, the latter requires a deeper exploration of the nature of creation and God's sovereign will. Even in natural suffering, Christians see opportunities for growth, compassion, and a deeper reliance on God.

The character of God in relation to human suffering is also illuminated by the incarnation of Jesus Christ. God's willingness to enter into the fullness of human experience, including pain and death, underscores His profound solidarity with humanity. Jesus's life and suffering serve as powerful demonstrations of how God uses even the direst circumstances to bring about greater goods, such as redemption and salvation.

Furthermore, the existence of free will and the presence of evil challenge us to consider the concept of eternal justice. Christian doctrine holds that this life is not the end but a precursor to an eternal existence. God's ultimate justice will rectify all wrongs, heal all wounds, and bring about a perfect equilibrium of mercy and righteousness. This hope does not invalidate current suffering but places it within a broader, hopeful perspective of redemption and restoration.

In the grand tapestry of existence, free will enables meaningful relationships based on love. Without it, not only would our relationship with God be deprived of love's significance, but our interactions with one another would lack depth and authenticity. The choices we make, for better or worse, shape our souls, influence the world, and move us along paths of either separation from or unity with the divine.

This perspective requires faith, a faith that believes in the ultimate goodness of God despite the shadows that loom large in our earthly experiences. It's a faith that recognizes our current understanding is limited, akin to seeing "through a glass, darkly" (1 Corinthians 13:12). The mysteries of suffering and evil, though daunting, do not negate God's love but remind us of the freedom we've been given and the responsibility that accompanies it.

The dynamics of free will and the problem of evil encourage Christians to act with compassion and empathy. In a world marred by suffering, believers are called to be agents of comfort, healing, and hope, reflecting God's love through their actions. These acts of kindness and solidarity are themselves powerful testimonies to the existence and nature of a loving God.

In confronting the problem of evil, therefore, we find not a barrier to faith but an invitation to deeper understanding and trust in God. It propels us into the heart of a divine mystery where love, freedom, and sovereignty coexist. Grappling with these issues is not an easy task, yet it is one that offers incredible insights into the character of God and the reality of human existence.

As we delve further into this exploration, let us approach the topic with open hearts and minds, seeking wisdom and understanding. The journey through questions of free will, suffering, and God's nature is challenging yet enriching, leading us towards a more profound faith and a closer relationship with the divine.

To conclude, the dialogue around free will and the nature of God is not merely academic but deeply personal. It touches on our deepest pains and highest hopes, urging us to look beyond the immediate to the eternal. In doing so, we discover not only the depths of God's love but also the incredible dignity and responsibility we hold as beings created in His image, capable of love, choice, and ultimately, of participating in the unfolding story of redemption.

May this exploration deepen your faith, enrich your understanding, and inspire you to engage with the world in a way that reflects the love and freedom at the core of your being. Remember, the presence of evil and suffering, though profoundly challenging, can lead us to a greater awareness of our need for God and foster a deeper appreciation for the gift of free will and the possibilities it opens for love and goodness in our lives.

Theodicies: Justifying God in the Face of Evil

Embarking on a journey to reconcile the existence of a benevolent, omnipotent God with the undeniable presence of evil in the world is perhaps one of the most profound endeavors a person of faith, or anyone on a spiritual quest, can undertake. This journey beckons us to delve deep into the realms of theology, philosophy, and the human condition, seeking answers to questions that have echoed through the ages.

The term 'theodicy' itself originates from two Greek words meaning 'God' and 'justice'. It is a concept that seeks to vindicate God in the face of evil's existence by proposing solutions that uphold God's goodness and omnipotence. Many have embarked on this quest, from ancient philosophers to modern theologians, each contributing their perspectives to this enduring mystery.

One essential perspective is the free will theodicy. At its heart, this view posits that God, in His ultimate wisdom and love, chose to create beings with free will - the freedom to choose between good and evil. This freedom is paramount to the existence of genuine love and moral goodness; without it, any 'good' actions would be robotic, devoid of meaning. But with this freedom comes the undeniable risk, and present reality, of evil.

The skeptic might question, "But couldn't God have created a world where free will exists yet evil does not?" It's a profound inquiry, leading us into deeper understanding. This question acknowledges the intrinsic value of free will while grappling with its consequences. It propels us into acknowledging that the depth of love, the richness of virtue, and the development of character are processes often born through struggles, pointing to a kind of moral and spiritual evolution that evil, paradoxically, makes possible.

Another significant perspective is the soul-making theodicy, forwarded by John Hick and others. This viewpoint suggests that God's purpose in allowing evil and suffering is for the development of souls into richer, more mature states of moral and spiritual quality. Life's adversities serve as a crucible, refining individuals and drawing forth virtues such as courage, perseverance, compassion, and humility.

Moreover, when we consider the concept of 'felicific calculus', proposed by philosophers like Jeremy Bentham, we find a utilitarian approach to understanding the presence of evil. It posits that the overall happiness or 'good' in the world outweighs the existence of evil, suggesting that God permits some evil for the sake of a greater good.

The narrative of Jesus Christ himself enters this conversation with paramount importance. The Christian belief in the incarnation, life, death, and resurrection of Jesus presents a God who is not distant from human suffering but intimately acquainted with it. God, in Christ, has entered into the very fabric of human agony, providing a presence that transforms suffering from within.

This divine solidarity with human suffering offers profound comfort and hope. It reassures us that our pain is neither meaningless nor unnoticed by God. Instead, it is embraced, shared, and ultimately redeemed. The cross stands as a testament that the darkest depths of evil and suffering can be the very place where God's love shines brightest.

However, the mystery of evil remains, and perhaps its full understanding is beyond human grasp. What is asked of us, then, is not a blind acquiescence but a faith that wrestles with doubt, questions that seek deeper understanding, and hearts that remain open to divine mystery, trusting in the goodness of God even when faced with the inexplicable.

In this journey, we also discover the importance of community and compassion. The presence of evil calls us not only to question but to action - to be bearers of light in the darkness, extending hands of support, voices of comfort, and acts of kindness. In doing so, we participate in the divine work of redeeming a broken world, embodying the very principles of love and goodness we seek to understand.

As we navigate the complex landscape of theodicies, let us do so with humility, acknowledging our limitations while embracing the pursuit of truth with courage and openness. The presence of evil in the world presents a profound challenge, one that prompts us to deeper faith, more profound understanding, and greater love.

Ultimately, our quest to justify God in the face of evil leads us back to the heart of what it means to be human and to live in relationship with the divine. It challenges us to live authentically in the tension between certainty and mystery, between the already and the not yet. In this sacred space, we find not only our deepest questions but also the seeds of hope, transformation, and renewal.

So, let us journey forth, not as those who have all the answers but as pilgrims who are guided by the light of faith, the compass of reason, and the map of tradition. Together, in community, with our eyes fixed on the example of Christ, we can navigate the paradox of a world marked by both profound beauty and unspeakable suffering. May our journey lead us into deeper fellowship with God and one another, grounding us in a hope that transcends our momentary trials and points us towards an eternal horizon where every tear will be wiped away, and love reigns supreme.

Chapter 5:
Christianity and Other Religions - Coexistence or Conflict?

In navigating the intricacies of global faith traditions, one finds Christianity at a crossroads between coexistence and conflict with other religions. This chapter delves into the defining nature of Christian faith - its exclusive truth claims juxtaposed with a call to love and dialogue that transcends borders of belief. Far from advocating a faith that isolates, Christianity, in its essence, encourages an engagement with the world that is both respectful and resolute. This stance is not about compromising the core of what Christians believe but about understanding that the strength of these beliefs can be the very foundation for meaningful dialogue with others. Interfaith encounters, when approached from a place of authenticity and humility, offer rich soil for growth and mutual understanding. They challenge us to articulate our faith more clearly and to listen deeply to the spiritual journeys of others, finding common ground without eroding the distinctive edges of our own convictions. Such interactions are not just possible; they are essential, offering a path through which faith can be a bridge rather than a barrier, a source of unity rather than division. As Christians, we are called to approach other religions not with a spirit of fear or superiority, but with a heart open to learn and a readiness to share the transformative hope that lies within us. This chapter invites readers to explore the dynamic between exclusivity and pluralism in Christianity, advocating for an approach that honors the truth claims of Christian faith while genuinely engaging in interfaith dialogue that respects and enriches all involved.

Exclusivity Vs. Pluralism: The Christian Claim

In embarking on this exploration of the delicate balance between exclusivity and pluralism, we enter into one of the Christian narrative's most nuanced and challenging areas. The discussion invites us to ponder deeply the essence of what Christianity claims concerning truth, salvation, and the nature of God's relationship with humanity across diverse cultural and religious landscapes.

The Christian claim, at its heart, asserts that there is an exclusive path to salvation through Jesus Christ. This declaration, encapsulated in scriptures such as John 14:6 where Jesus says, "I am the way and the truth and the life. No one comes to the Father except through me," might at first seem to stand at odds with the ideals of pluralism and the coexistence of multiple truths that characterizes much of modern thought.

However, this aspect of Christian faith doesn't negate the profound respect for the inherent worth and spiritual longing present within every individual, regardless of their faith background. Christianity, while holding to its truth-claims, also promotes a narrative of love, acceptance, and an earnest desire for every person to come to a realization of the truth as it sees it.

It is vital here to distinguish between the essence of Christianity's exclusivity and the misinterpretations that have sometimes led to divisiveness. The exclusivity claim should not be viewed as a tool for exclusion but as a declaration of the unique offer of salvation available in Jesus Christ. This offer, open to every human being, invites us into a relationship grounded in grace rather than merit.

This understanding calls us to approach dialogues with adherents of other faiths not with a spirit of triumphalism but with humility and a listener's heart. Engaging in respectful and meaningful conversations about our differences and similarities can bridge gaps and foster mutual respect.

In a world burgeoning with pluralistic ideologies, Christianity can seem like a solitary voice advocating for an absolute truth in a sea of relativism. Yet, this position does not necessitate conflict or coercion. Instead, it challenges Christians to exemplify love, the foundational principle of their faith, in every interaction and discourse.

This doesn't mean shying away from proclaiming the Christian message with confidence. On the contrary, it's about embodying the teachings of Christ, emphasizing the transformative power of love, and inviting others into this narrative through both word and deed.

The inclusivity inherent in Christian love necessitates an understanding and appreciation of other religious traditions and beliefs. Recognizing truths in other religions doesn't undermine Christianity's exclusivity claim but underscores the universality of certain human experiences and the widespread longing for connection with the Divine.

Moreover, the acknowledgment of common moral and ethical ground can serve as a foundation for constructive dialogue and cooperative action among different faith communities, aimed at addressing the myriad of global challenges we face today.

In navigating the tension between exclusivity and pluralism, Christians are called to a high standard of engagement. This involves earnestly wrestling with tough questions, embracing complexity, and seeking wisdom and guidance through prayer and study.

Ultimately, the Christian claim doesn't seek to diminish the rich tapestry of human spirituality but to offer a unique perspective on redemption and relationship with God. It's a perspective that Christians believe has the power to transform lives and bring hope in a world rife with despair.

As believers, the mandate to "go and make disciples of all nations" encompasses not only the proclamation of the gospel but living out its precepts through acts of service, kindness, and an unwavering commitment to justice and peace. This dual calling underscores the integration of faith and action, reflecting the holistic nature of Jesus' message.

In conclusion, the conversation around exclusivity and pluralism in the Christian context is not one that seeks to erect barriers but to invite open, honest exploration of faith's role in our lives and the world. It encourages Christians to be bearers of light, exemplars of unconditional love, and diligent seekers of truth, ever mindful of the dignity and worth of every person on their spiritual journey.

Thus, in embracing the Christian claim, we're called not only to affirm what we believe but to live it out in a way that draws others into a story of hope, transformation, and ultimate reconciliation with the Divine.

Interfaith Dialogue and Christian Truth Claims

In an increasingly pluralistic world, the question of how Christianity interacts with other religions is not merely academic—it's a pressing concern that affects interpersonal relationships, geopolitics, and personal faith journeys. At the heart of Christian engagement with other faiths is the question of truth. How can Christians remain committed to their own belief in the unique truth of the Gospel while engaging respectfully and meaningfully with other religious traditions? This section delves into the complexities of this question, exploring how interfaith dialogue can be a bridge rather than a barrier.

Firstly, it's vital to acknowledge that the landscape of religious interaction is markedly diverse. Christians encounter a spectrum of beliefs that, at times, may parallel moral teachings found within Christianity, and at other times, sharply diverge from the Christian worldview. This diversity necessitates a nuanced approach to dialogue—one that is rooted in humility and an earnest desire to understand the 'other.'

Such humility does not imply a dilution of one's faith. Rather, it is a recognition of our shared humanity and an acknowledgment that God's truth can shine through in unexpected ways, even beyond the bounds of the Christian tradition. This perspective allows Christians to engage in interfaith dialogue without the threat of relativism, firmly grounded in their assurance of the Gospel's truth while open to the insights and experiences of others.

At the core of Christianity are truth claims about the nature of God, human beings, and salvation—central among them, the belief in Jesus Christ as Lord and Savior. These claims are not merely philosophical propositions but are experienced as living realities by believers. Thus, when Christians enter into dialogue with adherents of other faiths, they do not merely share opinions but testify to a lived reality that shapes their entire being.

Dialogue, therefore, is not about winning arguments but about mutual encounter. It's an exchange where participants can share their deepest convictions with openness and vulnerability. For Christians, this means being ambassadors of Christ's love and grace, embodying the Gospel message through actions and words.

This approach requires a deep listening that goes beyond the surface, seeking to understand the meanings and experiences beneath the other's beliefs. Such deep listening can challenge our own assumptions and lead to greater self-understanding, as well as highlighting the profound connections that exist between all seekers of truth.

Interfaith dialogue also confronts Christians with challenging questions about their own faith. Engaging seriously with other religions compels us to articulate our beliefs more clearly and critically examine the reasons for our faith. This reflective process can strengthen our commitment and understanding, refining our ability to communicate the Gospel in a pluralistic world.

Moreover, interfaith engagement provides an opportunity to correct misunderstandings and combat stereotypes. Misconceptions about Christianity abound, just as misconceptions about other religions do. Through dialogue, we can break down barriers of ignorance and prejudice, revealing the true face of our faith—one marked by love, justice, and compassion.

It's also crucial to recognize the common ground that many religions share, such as values of compassion, peace, and justice. These shared values can serve as a foundation for collaborative efforts in addressing global challenges like poverty, injustice, and environmental degradation. By working together, followers of different faiths can witness to the power of religious conviction as a force for positive change in the world.

Yet, facing differences does not mean minimizing the distinctiveness of Christian claims. Christianity's insistence on the uniqueness of Christ as the way, the truth, and the life (John 14:6) remains a fundamental tenet that cannot be compromised. The challenge, then, is how to maintain this conviction while engaging respectfully and lovingly with those who hold to different ultimate truths.

This balance is not reached through easy solutions but through the hard work of genuine relationship-building and ongoing dialogue. It means creating spaces where difficult conversations can take place, where questions can be asked and wrestled with together, in a spirit of mutual respect and shared pilgrimage towards truth.

The New Testament provides a model for such engagement. The Apostle Paul, in his sermon at the Areopagus, acknowledges the religious devotion of the Athenians and uses it as a starting point to proclaim the Gospel (Acts 17:22-31). Paul does not compromise his message, but he connects with his audience by affirming their search for truth and pointing them towards Christ. This example illustrates how Christians can engage with other religions in a way that is both faithful to the Gospel and respectful of the other's sincere beliefs.

Ultimately, interfaith dialogue rooted in Christian convictions is an expression of hope. It is a testament to the belief that despite our deep differences, conversation is possible, understanding can grow, and love can flourish. This hope is not naive—it's grounded in the transformative power of the Gospel and the universal desire for truth and connection.

Therefore, as followers of Christ, we are called to approach interfaith dialogue with confidence in the truth of the Gospel, humility about our own understanding, and love for our neighbor, whatever their faith. By doing so, we bear witness to the reconciling love of God, inviting all people into the expansive embrace of divine grace.

In the journey of faith, engaging with other religions is not a detour or distraction but an integral part of living out the Gospel in a pluralistic world. It challenges us, enriches our faith, and deepens our commitment to living as Christ's ambassadors, agents of peace, and bearers of Good News. Let us, therefore, embrace the call to dialogue, trusting that in this sacred exchange, God is always at work, drawing us closer to the heart of divine mystery and the shared pursuit of ultimate truth.

Chapter 6:
The Reliability of Scripture - Textual Integrity and Transmission

In our journey of faith, understanding, and defense, one pivotal element that stands as both a foundation and a fortress is the reliability of Scripture. As we transcend the mere surface of our beliefs and delve into the profound depths of biblical texts, it becomes imperative to address the textual integrity and transmission of these ancient manuscripts. The endeavor to substantiate the Bible's historical trustworthiness confronts us with a myriad of manuscripts, each echoing the meticulous dedication of generations who have transmitted these sacred texts. It's a testament not just to the durability of mere words, but to the enduring power of Divine revelation, carried across centuries with astounding fidelity.

The canon of Scripture, encapsulating the divine symphony of God's revelation, stands as a beacon of truth amidst the ebb and flow of human history. This ensemble of texts, meticulously compiled, invites a discerning exploration of its development and significance - compelling evidence of its divine orchestration. In the grand tapestry of faith, the threads of textual integrity and canonical formation interweave, presenting a compelling narrative of divine perseverance. We are beckoned to not only admire the surface beauty of this tapestry but to also appreciate the intricate weaving together of history, tradition, and divine inspiration that underscores the unassailable reliability of Scripture. This journey into the depths of textual integrity and transmission does not erode our faith but enriches it, offering us firm ground upon which to stand as we navigate the complexities of the modern world. Embrace this exploration as an opportunity to fortify your understanding, embolden your faith, and eloquently articulate the enduring truth and relevance of Scripture in our lives.

Historical Trustworthiness of Biblical Texts

In the quest for truth and understanding, the historical trustworthiness of biblical texts stands as a beacon, inviting scrutiny and offering wisdom. It's a subject that bridges the past and present, asking us to consider not just the origins of these sacred writings, but their continued relevance in our lives today. For Christians and seekers alike, exploring the reliability of scripture is not just an academic exercise; it is a journey toward deeper faith and understanding.

The question of the Bible's historical trustworthiness often centers around the preservation of its texts over millennia. Here, we find a remarkable story of meticulous care and profound respect. The scribes who copied the ancient manuscripts did so with an awe-inspiring dedication to accuracy. Each word, each letter, was transcribed with precision, preserving the texts through generations.

This process of transmission illuminates the reverence with which these texts were held. The discovery of the Dead Sea Scrolls in the mid-20th century served to underscore the reliability of the biblical manuscripts. These ancient parchments, hidden in caves for over a millennium, matched the later manuscripts used in our Bibles today with striking similarity, affirming the careful stewardship of the Word over centuries.

Yet, the trustworthiness of the Bible is not anchored in manuscripts alone. Archaeology has lent a powerful voice to the historical credibility of biblical narratives. Time and again, excavations and analyses have confirmed the existence of places, cultures, and events described in scripture. From the ruins of Jericho to the palace of King David, the stones themselves bear witness to the Bible's historical grounding.

Moreover, the Bible's influence on literature, moral philosophy, and law throughout history underlines its profound impact on human civilization. Its teachings, parables, and commandments have shaped societies, inspired movements for social justice, and offered hope to countless individuals. This enduring relevance speaks to something beyond human authorship; it hints at a divine hand guiding its preservation and dissemination.

Critics often point to variations among manuscripts or the apparent contradictions within the biblical narrative. Yet, rather than undermining its trustworthiness, these elements invite deeper study and understanding. Scholars in textual criticism have shown that most variations are minor and do not affect the core teachings. The so-called contradictions often reveal different perspectives of the same truth, enriching our understanding rather than detracting from it.

Furthermore, the canonization process, while complex and historically contingent, was guided by principles of apostolic authority, orthodoxy, and widespread acceptance within the early Christian community. This wasn't arbitrary selection but a careful discernment of texts that were consistent with the apostolic teaching and were recognized by believers across different regions for their spiritual authority and authenticity.

It's essential, however, to approach the Bible not just as a historical document, but as a living text. Its power lies not only in its historical accuracy but in its ability to speak to our condition, offering guidance, wisdom, and hope. The stories of faith, resilience, and redemption found in its pages continue to resonate with readers, transcending cultural and temporal boundaries.

Engaging with the Bible critically and devotionally allows us to enter into a dialogue with the past, with each other, and with God. It requires an openness to be challenged and transformed by what we discover. The historical trustworthiness of the biblical texts serves as a foundation for this engagement, inviting us to trust, to question, and to seek deeper understanding.

In this spirit, the study of biblical texts becomes not just an intellectual pursuit but a spiritual journey. It encourages us to reflect on our beliefs, to wrestle with difficult questions, and to find our place within the ongoing story of faith. As we delve into the historical dimensions of scripture, we're not merely seeking facts; we're seeking connection, meaning, and truth.

As believers and seekers gather around these ancient texts, we find ourselves part of a community that spans millennia. The challenges, doubts, and aspirations that we bring to the Bible today are not so different from those of our ancestors in faith. This continuity of quest and questioning reflects the living nature of the Christian tradition, grounded in the historical trustworthiness of its scriptures yet always moving toward new horizons of understanding and application.

The journey toward affirming the reliability of the biblical texts is both personal and communal. It invites us to explore, to question, and ultimately, to stand in awe of the divine mystery that speaks through scripture. In its pages, we encounter a God who is both beyond and within history, whose truth transcends time even as it engages directly with our lives.

In a world hungry for meaning and connection, the historical trustworthiness of the Bible offers a foundation upon which to build our understanding of ourselves, our world, and our God. It challenges us to look beyond the surface, to delve into the depths of faith, and to embrace the transformative power of the Word. As we journey through scripture, let us do so with hearts open to receive, minds prepared to be challenged, and spirits willing to be stirred.

The exploration of the Bible's historical trustworthiness is not an endpoint but a gateway. It opens up avenues for deeper exploration of faith, ethics, and the human condition. This journey invites us to a richer, more nuanced understanding of Christianity and its sacred texts, challenging us to live out our faith with integrity, compassion, and a commitment to truth.

In the final analysis, the trustworthiness of biblical texts beckons us to a faith that is informed, resilient, and vibrant. It calls us to be seekers of truth and bearers of light in a world that often dwells in shadows. Let us then approach the sacred scriptures with both reverence and critical inquiry, allowing them to guide us toward wisdom, understanding, and a deeper, more abiding faith.

The Canon: Development and Significance

In exploring the reliability of Scripture, it becomes fundamental to address the formation and significance of the canonical books. The canon, comprising the books deemed divinely inspired and authoritative for faith and doctrine in Christianity, has a journey of development marked by divine guidance, historical discernment, and communal affirmation.

The process by which these texts were acknowledged transcends a mere historical occurrence; it unveils a profound narrative of faithfulness and deliberation within the early Christian community. This community sought not to arbitrarily select texts, but to recognize those writings that echoed the authentic voice of God—a voice they had experienced in Christ and His resurrection, which remains the cornerstone of Christian faith.

The criteria for canonicity were neither arbitrary nor superficial. Texts were evaluated based on apostolic authorship, congruency with the received faith, and their widespread acceptance and use in liturgical and doctrinal instruction among the early churches. This discernment process was illuminated by the Holy Spirit, enabling the community to distinguish texts that bore the true hallmarks of divine inspiration.

The development of the canon was, therefore, not an instantaneous event but a progressive journey. This journey was driven by the need to preserve the authentic apostolic teaching amidst rising heresies and to provide a standardized set of texts for liturgical use across the diverging congregations of Christianity's infancy.

What's more, the canon's formation was an intimate part of Christianity's response to skepticism and persecution. In a world that often demanded renunciation of faith under pain of death, the early Christians found in these texts a source of spiritual strength, communal identity, and theological clarity.

Understanding the significance of the canon extends beyond acknowledging its historical development; it involves recognizing its role in shaping the identity and theology of Christian faith through the centuries. The canon has equipped believers to navigate the challenges of their times with wisdom and grace drawn from the depths of sacred scripture.

The integrity of the canon assures us that what we have today remains a reliable witness to God's revelation in Jesus Christ. The meticulous care and spiritual discernment that guided the early church in recognizing these texts stand as a testament to their authenticity and authority.

Moreover, the canonical scriptures invite believers into a transformative engagement with the Word of God. They are not simply historical documents, but living words that continue to speak into our lives, guiding, challenging, and comforting us. Through them, the Spirit speaks, making the ancient words freshly relevant in contemporary life.

The canon's development also speaks to the unity in diversity that characterizes the Christian faith. Across the spectrum of Christian traditions, the canon is a shared foundation, a common ground from which dialogue and understanding can emerge. It is a unifying thread that binds together a diverse global faith community.

Additionally, the history of the canon challenges Christians to appreciate the depth and breadth of the heritage of faith. It invites an exploration of how early Christians lived, believed, and upheld the teachings of Jesus in contexts often hostile to their message. This historical engagement enriches contemporary faith, providing examples of courage, faithfulness, and theological reflection.

In a world where truth is often seen as subjective, the canon stands as a beacon of divine revelation. It asserts the possibility of knowing truth—ultimate truth that has the power to liberate, transform, and redeem. In its pages, seekers find the narrative of God's action in history, culminating in the life, death, and resurrection of Jesus Christ for the salvation of humanity.

For those exploring Christianity, understanding the canon's formation is vital. It reveals not just a list of books but a story of divine and human interaction that invites each person into a life-changing relationship with God. The canon's existence reassures us of a God who communicates, who has spoken and continues to speak through the scriptures.

Reflecting on the canon's development and significance, believers are called to a deeper faith and a renewed commitment to engaging with Scripture. It invites a journey of discovery, where the ancient texts illuminate paths for living faithfully in a complex and rapidly changing world.

In embracing the canon, Christians find not only the roots of their faith but also the wings to explore its limitless horizons. It is a compass for spiritual navigation, offering direction and purpose in the pursuit of truth, justice, and love. The canonical texts beckon us to journey deeper into the heart of God, where we find the courage to face life's challenges and the inspiration to transform our world.

As we continue to explore the reliability of Scripture, let us do so with a profound respect for the process that has preserved these texts for us. The canon's development is a cornerstone of our faith, offering a foundation upon which we can confidently build our understanding of God, ourselves, and the world around us. It stands as a testament to the enduring nature of divine revelation and the persistent quest for truth that defines the Christian journey.

Chapter 7:
Morality and Ethics - Absolute or Relative?

In our journey through understanding and defending the Christian faith against modern skepticism, we encounter the undulating terrain of morality and ethics. Is there a universal moral law that transcends time and culture, or are our ethical standards merely a product of societal consensus and change with the tide of public opinion? This chapter delves into the heart of this debate, asserting that the existence of objective moral values points us towards a moral Lawgiver. It's undeniable that across civilizations and epochs, certain truths - such as justice, compassion, and integrity - have been upheld as virtuous. This consistency echoes the Christian doctrine that humanity is imbued with the knowledge of right and wrong, a reflection of the Creator's moral nature. Moreover, in a world increasingly embracing moral relativism, the need for Christians to understand and articulate the basis of biblical ethics in contemporary discussions becomes ever more critical. Through reasoned arguments and heartfelt conviction, we'll explore how Christian morality isn't just a set of rules imposed from on high but a path to true freedom and flourishing, rooted in the unchanging character of God.

The Moral Argument for God's Existence

In traversing the landscape of morality and ethics, one of the most compelling territories we explore is the moral argument for the existence of God. This argument asserts that if there are objective moral values, then God must exist. It's a journey not just of logic and philosophy but of deep, personal introspection. At its core, this argument invites us to consider the origin of the moral compass that guides our decisions and judgments.

Let's start with the assertion that our universe is governed by laws, both physical and moral. Much like the law of gravity is an undeniable force in the physical realm, the presence of a moral law that we feel compelled to follow suggests an authoritative source. This moral law exists beyond personal and cultural differences, suggesting an origin that is universal and absolute.

The presence of objective moral values points towards a reality that transcends our individual subjective experiences. Consider for a moment a world without these objective values; it would be a reality where concepts of right and wrong, justice and injustice, are mere social constructs, as malleable as clay. Yet, deep within us, there is a recognition that certain things are inherently wrong, such as torture or racial discrimination, regardless of our cultural upbringing or personal preferences. This inherent understanding suggests a moral blueprint imprinted upon humanity.

Faced with the undeniable, forceful stream of objective moral values, one might wonder about its source. Such universal values demand a universal lawgiver. This is where the concept of God enters the conversation—not merely as a creator of the cosmos but as the author of morality itself. The idea posits that without a divine moral lawgiver, objective moral values and duties would not exist.

Some may argue that moral values can be derived from evolutionary processes or social contracts developed for mutual benefit. However, this perspective falls short when we consider the depth and universality of moral obligations. Evolution and social contracts might explain human behaviors and tendencies, but they do not account for the moral oughtness—the compelling sense that we ought to do some things and ought not to do others, independent of our desires or survival needs.

This moral oughtness, an intrinsic part of the human experience, aligns with the notion of being made in the image of a moral God. It speaks to a purpose and design inherent in our very being, a call to rise above mere survival instincts and engage with ethical values that point beyond ourselves.

Engaging with the moral argument for God's existence challenges us to examine the foundations of our moral convictions. Are they merely the product of impersonal forces and social agreements, or do they speak to a higher order and purpose? If moral values truly are objective and universal, their best explanation is the existence of a moral lawgiver, God, who embodies and is the source of these values.

The beauty of this argument lies not in the dismissal of alternative explanations for morality, but in its invitation to explore the deepest layers of meaning and purpose in our lives. It invites a reflection on the transcendent, on something greater than ourselves, which imbues our lives with inherent value and significance.

At a practical level, the moral argument for God's existence offers a robust foundation for moral action. In a world that increasingly leans towards relativism, this argument anchors us to a moral standard that transcends changing societal norms and preferences. It calls us to a higher duty, to live in alignment with a moral order that reflects the character and nature of God.

This argument does not stand in isolation but complements other discussions around the existence of God, such as the cosmological and teleological arguments. Together, they weave a tapestry of reasoning that points to a coherent understanding of a personal, moral, and creative God. These reflections are not mere intellectual exercises but are integral to how we live out our faith and engage with the world around us.

For Christians, the moral argument reinforces the view of human beings as morally responsible agents, called to live in a manner that reflects God's moral excellence. It affirms the intrinsic worth of every person, grounded in being created in the image of a moral God.

In engaging with skeptics and seekers, this argument offers a bridge built on the common ground of our moral intuitions. It invites a conversation not just about beliefs but about what it means to be human and the source of our moral convictions. In a world searching for meaning, it positions Christianity as a faith that provides cogent answers to our deepest moral questions.

Ultimately, the moral argument for God's existence beckons us towards a discovery of the divine source of morality. It challenges us to reflect on the nature of good and evil, right and wrong, and to consider the profound implications of a universe created with purpose, meaning, and moral order. It's an invitation to embark on a journey not only of the mind but of the heart, towards a deeper understanding and relationship with the moral lawgiver, God Himself.

In conclusion, the moral argument offers a compelling case for the existence of God, grounding objective moral values in a transcendent, personal source. It enriches our understanding of the relationship between morality and divinity, calling us to live lives reflective of the ultimate source of goodness and truth. As we navigate the complexities of modern ethical discussions, this argument stands as a beacon of hope, affirming that our deepest moral intuitions point us towards a reality that is both meaningful and divinely ordained.

Biblical Ethics in Contemporary Society

In navigating the complexities of modern life, we encounter a myriad of moral dilemmas that challenge our understanding and application of ethical principles. This is where the timeless teachings of the Bible come into play, offering guidance that transcends epochs and cultures. As we delve into the intersection of Biblical ethics and contemporary society, it's crucial to recognize that these divine precepts are not just ancient texts but living, breathing instructions that illuminate our path towards righteousness.

The world we live in is vastly different from the one the authors of the Bible inhabited. Technology, social norms, and knowledge have evolved in ways unimaginable to the ancients. Yet, the moral fabric that constitutes the core of Biblical ethics—love, justice, compassion, integrity—remains relevant, guiding us in confronting modern challenges with wisdom and courage.

Consider the principle of love, epitomized by the commandment to "love your neighbor as yourself" (Mark 12:31). This foundational pillar transcends time and culture, urging us to extend kindness and understanding to all, regardless of our differences. In a world fragmented by divisions, the radical call to love serves as a powerful antidote to hatred and prejudice, fostering unity and peace.

Similarly, the Biblical emphasis on justice speaks directly to the heart of contemporary societal issues. From advocating for the marginalized to challenging unjust systems, Scripture compels us to be agents of change, working tirelessly to create a world that reflects God's justice and righteousness. In doing so, we're called not only to address the symptoms of injustice but to confront its root causes, embodying the prophetic vision of a society founded on equity and compassion.

In facing the vast, complicated web of modern life, the Biblical command to exercise compassion offers a beacon of hope.

Compassion isn't merely an emotional response; it's an active force that motivates us to alleviate suffering and extend assistance to those in need. Whether through personal acts of kindness or participation in broader movements for social change, our compassionate actions embody the loving heart of God in a world desperate for hope.

Integrity, as highlighted throughout Scripture, equips us to navigate the ethical complexities of contemporary society with honesty and moral clarity. In a culture often marked by relativism and deceit, the Biblical call to integrity challenges us to be people of our word, living out our convictions with consistency and courage, even when doing so requires personal sacrifice.

The issue of environmental stewardship provides a poignant example of Biblical ethics applied to a modern dilemma. The Scriptural mandate to care for creation (Genesis 2:15) urges us to confront issues like climate change and environmental degradation, not as political issues, but as moral imperatives rooted in our responsibility as caretakers of God's creation.

Moreover, the sphere of economics and business ethics is another area where Biblical principles offer profound insights. The denouncement of greed and the call for fairness and generosity in economic dealings (Proverbs 11:1; Luke 12:15) challenge us to rethink our engagement with the modern economy, advocating for practices that promote human flourishing over mere profit.

In the realm of politics and governance, Biblical ethics guide us towards principles of leadership characterized by servant-hood and humility (Mark 10:42-45), marking a stark contrast to the often power-hungry framework of contemporary politics. These teachings invite those in positions of authority to prioritize the welfare of the people they serve, fostering societies marked by justice and care for the vulnerable.

The sanctity of life, a principle deeply embedded in Scripture, speaks directly to contentious issues like abortion and euthanasia in today's society. By affirming the inherent worth of every human being, created in the image of God (Genesis 1:27), Biblical ethics demand a rigorous defense of life, advocating for policies and practices that protect and honor the most vulnerable among us.

In matters of personal moral conduct—issues like honesty, sexual integrity, and the stewardship of our bodies—the Bible provides clear guidance that, when applied, offer a counter-cultural narrative to the prevailing norms of contemporary society. These teachings challenge us to consider the long-term implications of our choices, aligning our lives with a Biblical worldview that honors God and respects others.

Confronting the ethical challenges of modern technology, including issues like privacy, data ethics, and the exponential growth of artificial intelligence, requires us to apply Scriptural principles in discerning and innovative ways. The wisdom of Scripture, though ancient, provides an ethical framework that guides us in making moral decisions in these uncharted territories, ensuring that our advancements serve to uplift humanity rather than diminish it.

As we navigate the complex landscapes of social justice, the Biblical calls for empathy, solidarity, and action inspire us to stand alongside those fighting against oppression and inequality. Scripture implores us to listen to the voices of the marginalized, joining hands across divides to build a more just and inclusive society.

The journey of integrating Biblical ethics into contemporary society is both a challenge and an opportunity. It prompts us to engage deeply with Scripture, wrestling with its teachings and discerning their application in our lives today. As we do so, we discover that the Bible is not a relic of the past but a living guide that continually speaks into our present, offering wisdom, encouragement, and direction for the journey ahead.

In a world hungry for moral guidance and spiritual depth, the teachings of Scripture stand as a beacon of hope and truth. By embracing and living out Biblical ethics, we bear witness to the transformative power of God's Word, challenging and changing the world one decision at a time. Let us, therefore, commit to this high calling, endeavoring to model a way of life that reflects the beauty, goodness, and truth of the Gospel, illuminating the path for others to follow.

Chapter 8:
The Resurrection - Cornerstone of Christian Belief

In traversing the landscapes of Christian doctrine, the resurrection stands as the paramount miracle, the lynchpin of Christian faith that affirms Jesus is who He claimed to be. It's not merely another story in the anthology of religious miracles but the foundation upon which all other beliefs are laid. Skeptics have scrutinized it, historians have debated it, and believers have clung to it, finding in its account not just hope for an afterlife but the embodiment of victory over death itself. This event is not just a claim of Christianity; it is its very heartbeat. Without the resurrection, Christianity crumbles under the weight of its promises, but with it, the faith shines as a beacon of hope, transcending the confines of history to touch the lives of millions. We've ventured through discussions on the reliability of scripture, the harmonization of faith and reason, and the tackling of moral quandaries, all of which are pillars in their own right. Yet, it is the resurrection that casts the longest shadow, affirming the power of God and setting Christianity apart as a faith not just in teachings or ethical principles, but in a living person. Through rigorous examination of historical evidence and thoughtful engagement with alternative theories, this chapter seeks not just to defend a pivotal event but to invite readers into the transformative reality it represents. It's a call to view the resurrection not as a distant historical occurrence but as the turning point in a narrative that invites each individual into a journey of faith, hope, and love.

Historical Evidence for the Resurrection

The resurrection of Jesus stands as the cornerstone of Christian belief, a foundation upon which the faith asserts its uniqueness and power. It's in exploring this remarkable claim that one embarks on a journey not just of faith, but of reason, historical analysis, and the exploration of evidence that challenges the boundaries of belief and skepticism alike.

At the heart of Christianity is the resurrection, an event that is unparalleled in human history. It's a claim that, if true, not only confirms the divinity of Jesus but also offers hope and redemption to humanity. Thus, understanding the historical evidence for the resurrection is not just an academic exercise; it's a pursuit that touches the essence of what it means to believe.

Firstly, let's consider the accounts of the resurrection itself. The Gospels of Matthew, Mark, Luke, and John, despite their variations, converge on the fundamental details of the resurrection. Skeptics often argue these variations detract from their reliability, yet in historical analysis, such discrepancies are expected in genuine eyewitness accounts, indicating that the writers were not colluding but independently reporting events as they remembered or understood them.

Furthermore, the presence of women as the first witnesses to the resurrection in all four Gospel accounts is noteworthy. In the cultural and historical context of the time, women were not considered credible witnesses in legal proceedings. The inclusion of women as primary witnesses to such a pivotal event is an element that most fabricators seeking to convince a skeptical audience would likely avoid. This lends an air of authenticity to the narrative, suggesting that the accounts were more concerned with reporting witnessed events than conforming to the expectations of the era.

Moving beyond the biblical texts, we delve into extrabiblical sources that reference Jesus and the early Christian movement. Authors like Flavius Josephus, Tacitus, and Pliny the Younger, though not proponents of Christianity, provide corroborative accounts that affirm the existence of Jesus and the early Christians' belief in his resurrection. These accounts are crucial as they come from external sources not vested in promoting Christianity.

The exponential growth of early Christianity under the heavy persecution of the Roman Empire also speaks volumes. The willing acceptance of martyrdom by the apostles and early Christians makes sense only within the context of a profound conviction in the truth of the resurrection. People do not readily choose death for what they know to be a lie. This transformation from fear to unwavering faith strongly supports the reality of the resurrection experience.

Historically, the empty tomb serves as another significant piece of evidence. The fact that the location of Jesus' tomb was known to Christians and non-Christians alike and that no one in the first century produced Jesus' body to quash the burgeoning Christian movement indicates that the tomb was indeed empty. Skeptics at the time did not deny the empty tomb; rather, they proposed alternative explanations, such as theft, which inadvertently supports the disciples' claims.

Additionally, the Jewish Sabbath was changed from Saturday to Sunday by early Christians to honor the day of Jesus' resurrection. Such a profound change in a deeply ingrained religious practice underscores the impact and significance of the resurrection event, further attesting to its authenticity in the minds of the earliest followers of Jesus.

The transformation of Saul of Tarsus, a zealous persecutor of Christians, into Paul the Apostle, one of Christianity's most prolific messengers, is yet another striking evidence. Paul's dramatic conversion, prompted by a revelatory experience of the risen Jesus, initiated a life of hardship and dedication to spreading the message of Christ. His epistles, which form a significant portion of the New Testament, offer both theological insights and early testimonials of the resurrection.

Moreover, the existence of early Christian creeds within the New Testament texts, like that in 1 Corinthians 15:3-7, presents a summary of resurrection appearances that Paul cites as being delivered to him. This creed is widely dated by scholars to within a few years of Jesus' death, suggesting a very early belief in the resurrection that was transmitted among Jesus' followers.

When taken together, these strands of evidence—biblical accounts, extrabiblical attestations, cultural and societal shifts, and personal transformations—form a compelling argument for the historical reality of the resurrection. It is an event that does not merely rest on the foundation of faith but is also supported by a critical examination of historical data.

Engaging with the historical evidence for the resurrection challenges us to reconsider the boundaries between history and faith, evidence and belief. It propels us into a deeper understanding of the transformative power of the resurrection, not only as an historical event but as a living reality that continues to inspire, challenge, and offer hope to millions worldwide.

The resurrection's historical plausibility provides a solid ground for faith that is not blind but informed; it encourages a belief that engages the mind as well as the heart. In the face of skepticism and doubt, the historical evidence for the resurrection stands as a beacon of hope, affirming the power of truth, the promise of renewal, and the profound depth of God's love for humanity.

As we continue to explore and understand the evidence of the resurrection, we do so with the knowledge that our faith is rooted not just in spiritual convictions but in the historical reality of an event that has forever altered the course of human history. The resurrection is not just a foundational doctrine of Christianity; it is a testament to the eternal love and power of God, a source of endless inspiration, hope, and transformation for all who seek to understand its truth.

Answering Alternative Theories

In our journey to understand the cornerstone of Christian belief, it's essential to navigate through the sea of alternative theories that challenge the historicity of the Resurrection. These theories, while varied in their nature, share a common goal: to provide explanations that diverge from the miraculous intervention of God. It's crucial, then, for believers and seekers alike, to critically assess these alternatives, not to dismiss them outright, but to seek the truth with an open heart and mind.

Among the most popular of these theories is the Swoon Theory, suggesting that Jesus did not actually die on the cross but was merely unconscious when taken down and later revived in the tomb. This theory, while initially appealing to naturalistic preferences, falls short under historical and medical scrutiny. The Roman executioners were experts in death; their entire profession revolved around ensuring that their subjects did not survive. Moreover, the accounts of Jesus' post-resurrection appearances in multiple and independent sources show him interacting in ways that would be impossible for someone recovering from such trauma.

Another theory posits that the disciples stole Jesus' body, thereby fabricating the Resurrection narrative. This theory, however, struggles against the psychological and sociological realities of the disciples' behavior. Followers of Jesus were transformed from despairing, fearful individuals into bold proclaimers of the Resurrection, willing to face persecution and death. It's challenging to reconcile this radical transformation with the notion that they were actively perpetuating a fraud.

A variation on this theme suggests that it was not the disciples, but grave robbers who removed Jesus' body. Yet, this theory does not account for the profound experiences of the Resurrection encountered by the disciples and others, recorded in multiple, independent early sources. Grave robbery cannot explain the appearances of Jesus or the empty tomb's power to inspire a global movement based on the belief in the Resurrection.

The Hallucination Theory offers a psychological explanation, proposing that the experiences of the Risen Christ were subjective visions or hallucinations. While addressing the personal nature of the appearances, this theory fails to explain the group experiences, the empty tomb, and the diversity of individuals who encountered the Risen Jesus. Hallucinations are typically singular, highly subjective, and do not lead to the kind of consistent, life-altering behavior displayed by the followers of Jesus.

Another approach argues that the Resurrection narrative resulted from mythologization or legendary development over time. This view contends that the accounts of Jesus rising from the dead are later embellishments. However, the timeline for the development of the Gospels and Paul's letters suggests a period too brief for myth to significantly alter historical events. Furthermore, these documents show concern for historical details and corroborate each other in ways uncharacteristic of myth.

To engage with these theories meaningfully, it's paramount to adhere to principles of critical thinking and historical analysis. Evaluating the available evidence, the context of early Christianity, and the motivations and behaviors of its adherents offers a robust framework through which to understand the claims of the Resurrection.

Moreover, the transformative power of the belief in the Resurrection cannot be understated. It's improbable that a movement based on deceit or hallucinations would have the profound, enduring, and positive impact seen in the lives of billions over millennia. The moral and ethical teachings of Jesus, centered on love, forgiveness, and peace, further lend credence to the authenticity of the Resurrection event as the foundation of Christian faith.

In dialogues with skeptics and seekers, it's beneficial to approach these discussions with humility and respect. The journey to faith is deeply personal, and while reasoned arguments and evidence play crucial roles, the experience of God's presence and love remains central. Our engagement with alternative theories should, therefore, be both an intellectual and a spiritual exercise.

Finally, it's vital to remember that faith, while informed by evidence and reason, transcends them. The Resurrection, as the cornerstone of Christian belief, invites us into a relationship with the living God. It challenges us to view the world and our lives through the lens of hope and redemption. This transformative invitation opens the door to experiencing the profound love and grace offered through Jesus Christ.

In conclusion, while alternative theories to the Resurrection merit consideration and provide avenues for discussion, they ultimately fall short in explaining the full scope of evidence and the transformative power of the Resurrection. As we continue to seek understanding and engage with others on this topic, let us do so with a spirit of grace, always pointing back to the love and hope found in Christ. Thus, in answering these alternative theories, we not only defend a historical event but proclaim a living truth that continues to change lives today.

Chapter 9:
Creation, Evolution, and Christianity

In navigating the delicate dance between the divine act of Creation and the scientific theory of Evolution, we find ourselves at a crossroads that seemingly divides faith and reason. Yet, it is in this intersection that Christianity can offer a profound and unifying perspective. The genesis of the universe, illuminated by the light of science, isn't a battleground for ideological supremacy but rather a fertile ground for harmony. Understanding Genesis in the context of modern scientific discoveries does not diminish the awe of Creation; instead, it enriches our comprehension of the omnipotence of God, who set forth the laws of nature that guide the evolutionary process. The debate surrounding Evolution within Christian doctrine often stems from a misunderstanding of both scientific theory and theological narrative. It's essential to recognize that faith and science are not mutually exclusive but are complementary ways of understanding the world around us. This chapter aims to illustrate that Christianity, far from being at odds with Evolution, provides a framework within which the marvels of Creation and the empirical observations of science can coexist. As Christians, embracing this synthesis not only strengthens our faith but also empowers us to engage in thoughtful dialogue with the broader scientific community, showcasing a faith that is rational, open, and deeply connected with the wonders of the natural world.

Understanding Genesis in the Light of Science

In embarking on the quest for harmony between the narrative of Genesis and the discoveries of modern science, it is essential to approach with both humility and an eagerness for understanding. The interplay between faith and reason is not a battleground but a fertile field where knowledge and belief can coexist and enrich one another. The opening chapters of the Bible, often the center of debate, hold deep spiritual truths not bound by the constraints of human empirical observation. They invite believers into a profound understanding of God's relationship with the world.

When delving into Genesis, it's crucial to acknowledge that the biblical texts were written in a context vastly different from our own. These ancient narratives were communicated to people who understood the world through a lens that did not involve the scientific method or empirical observation in the way we comprehend them today. The purpose of these texts was not to provide a detailed account of the material origins of the universe, but to convey profound truths about God, humanity, and our place in the cosmos.

Science, in its pursuit of understanding the physical universe, employs observation, experimentation, and reasoning. It gives us a remarkable window into the processes and laws that govern existence. Through scientific inquiry, we uncover the beauty and complexity of the cosmos, from the unimaginable vastness of galaxies to the intricate details of DNA. These discoveries inspire awe and wonder and often resonate with the biblical affirmation of the goodness and majesty of God's creation.

One of the key areas where Genesis and science have been perceived to clash is in the account of creation. The six-day creation narrative has been a point of contention, with some reading it as a literal chronological account. However, an alternative approach is to see these days as a literary framework, a poetic device that conveys theological truths about God's creative authority and intentionality. This perspective allows for the acknowledgment of scientific theories, such as the Big Bang and evolution, as insights into the means by which God brought about the diversity and complexity of life.

The concept of humanity made in the image of God — imago Dei — is central to the Judeo-Christian understanding of human dignity and value. This theological claim stands beautifully alongside the scientific exploration of human origins. It does not conflict with the evidence for human evolution but enriches it by providing a profound reason for the unique capacities of humans for relationship, morality, and creativity.

Genesis also speaks to the stewardship of creation, a mandate that finds new urgency in our growing awareness of environmental issues through scientific study. When science shows us the fragility of our planet and the impact of human activity on its ecosystems, believers are reminded of their responsibility to care for God's creation, not out of mere utility, but as a sacred duty to the Creator.

An exploration of the flood narrative through scientific lenses offers insights into ancient Near Eastern cataclysms that could have inspired such stories. Rather than seeking to prove a global flood in scientific terms, understanding these accounts in their historical and cultural context can reveal how God communicates through the mediums and understandings available to people at the time. It's an invitation to see God's actions and intentions woven through the fabric of history, teaching us lessons of judgment, mercy, and redemption.

It is vital for believers to approach these intersections of faith and science with openness to learn and grow. The pursuit of scientific knowledge, much like the pursuit of spiritual understanding, is a journey marked by wonder, questioning, and awe. Both realms of inquiry bring us closer to truth, each complementing the other in a harmonious dance that enriches our comprehension of the divine narrative.

Conversations between the realms of faith and science are often marked by mutual respect and a shared sense of mystery. Many scientists, some of them devout Christians, view their work as a form of worship, an exploration of the intricacy and majesty of God's creation. Their insights do not diminish the wonder of faith but illuminate it, offering new dimensions of appreciation for the works of the Creator.

In the endeavor to reconcile Genesis with science, it is also important to recognize the limits of human understanding. Both faith and science are human endeavors, striving to grasp realities beyond our full comprehension. This humility opens the space for dialogue, for asking questions, and for exploring the depths of both the material and spiritual realms without fear. It means accepting that mystery is an essential part of both faith and scientific inquiry.

Engaging with Genesis in the light of science challenges believers to expand their understanding of God's revelation. It encourages a faith that is not fragile, threatened by new discoveries or different interpretations, but is robust, dynamic, and open to the vastness of God's truth. This approach fosters a Christianity that is intellectually engaging, spiritually enriching, and relevant in a scientifically informed age.

As followers of Christ in the modern world, embracing the dialogue between Genesis and science is part of our witness. It demonstrates a belief in a God who is big enough to encompass all truth, whether revealed through Scripture or through creation itself. It reflects a faith that is not in opposition to reason but is enriched by it, offering a comprehensive understanding of reality that speaks to both the heart and the mind.

Finally, understanding Genesis in the light of science is an ongoing journey, not a destination. It involves continuous learning, questioning, and marveling at the mystery and beauty of God's work in the universe. It is an invitation to an ever-deeper understanding of the divine, a pursuit that unites heart and mind in awe of the Creator. In this journey, believers are equipped not only with knowledge but with a faith that engages the world with confidence, compassion, and conviction.

Let us, therefore, approach this journey with open hearts and minds, eager to discover the wonders of God's creation afresh. Let us engage with science not as a threat but as a conversation partner, through which God can reveal the depths of his wisdom and creativity. In doing so, we embody a faith that resonates with truth and love, inviting all who seek to know more of the mystery and majesty of our Creator.

The Evolution Debate: Compatibility with Christian Doctrine

In delving into the intricate relationship between the theory of evolution and Christian doctrine, we enter a realm replete with intellectual challenge, spiritual reflection, and boundless opportunities for growth. The debate surrounding evolution and Christianity often evokes passionate responses, not merely because of the scientific implications but, more importantly, due to the profound spiritual questions it raises. As we explore this terrain, our intent is not to provide definitive answers to all questions but to illuminate paths through which faith and science can coexist harmoniously.

At the heart of this discussion lies the profound and beautiful narrative of Genesis. Often, interpretations of this sacred text focus on a literalistic understanding, which can lead to the perception of a chasm between faith and evolutionary science. Yet, when we approach Scripture not just as a historical account but as a profound exploration of God's relationship with creation, new dimensions of understanding can emerge. Viewing Genesis through this lens, we can appreciate the poetic and theological truths it conveys without feeling compelled to reject scientific explanations of the universe's origin.

Understanding evolution as a mechanism of creation allows us to marvel at the complexity and beauty of God's world in a new light. This perspective does not diminish the divine but rather expands our appreciation for the intricate intelligence and creativity of the Creator. It beckons us to explore the natural world with reverence, seeing in it the handiwork of an artist whose palette encompasses the genes and ecosystems that give rise to life's diversity.

It's also crucial to address the misunderstandings that fuel much of the debate. Some argue that evolution undermines the special status of humans made in the image of God. However, understanding our biological origins in the context of evolution can actually enhance our appreciation for the unique spiritual and moral capacities that distinguish humanity. This view does not detract from our significance but invites a deeper reflection on what it means to be created in God's image.

Furthermore, the compatibility between evolution and Christian doctrine can be seen in the way both realms invite us to a posture of humility and wonder. Scientific inquiry, at its best, is a process of seeking truth through observation, experimentation, and critical thinking. Similarly, faith involves a journey of seeking understanding, guided by Scripture, tradition, reason, and experience. Both paths require an openness to revising our understandings in the light of new knowledge and insights.

One of the most profound ways in which Christianity and evolution can be reconciled is through the concept of co-creation. This idea posits that God's creative activity is ongoing and that evolution is one of the processes through which God continues to bring forth the abundance of life. This perspective imbues the evolutionary process with a sacred purpose, inviting believers to recognize God's presence in the gradual unfolding of creation's complexity.

In the discussions between faith and science, we must avoid the trap of false dichotomies. Too often, the debate is framed as a choice between faith and reason, or between scripture and science. This binary thinking limits our understanding and prevents us from embracing a more holistic view of our world and our place in it. Christian doctrine, properly understood, is not in opposition to scientific discovery but can enrich our understanding of it, just as science can illuminate aspects of the divine.

To navigate the evolution debate within Christian circles, we must cultivate a spirit of dialogue and openness. This involves listening to differing perspectives with respect, seeking common ground, and acknowledging the limits of our understanding. It requires a commitment to education, both in the intricacies of scientific theories and in the depth of theological thought. By doing so, we can move beyond contention and towards a more integrated understanding of faith and science.

The evolution debate also challenges Christians to expand their vision of divine action in the world. Rather than seeing God's hand only in miraculous interventions that defy natural laws, we can recognize divine creativity and guidance within the processes that science explores, including evolution. This view allows us to see God not as distant and detached, waiting to intervene sporadically, but as intimately involved in the ongoing creation and development of life.

Moreover, this conversation about evolution and Christian doctrine has ethical implications. It reminds us of our responsibility as stewards of creation. If we understand the natural world as a product of divine creativity, our role is not to exploit but to care for and protect it. This stewardship is grounded in a theology that sees the entire cosmos as an expression of God's love and creativity, a precious gift entrusted to our care.

Embracing the compatibility between evolution and Christian doctrine also has profound pastoral implications. It offers a way for Christians who are also scientists or those struggling with doubts about their faith in light of scientific knowledge to integrate their spiritual and intellectual lives. This reconciliation could be a source of strength, providing a foundation for a faith that is both intellectually robust and deeply spiritual.

Finally, the dialogue between Christianity and the theory of evolution represents an opportunity for witnessing to the world. In a society where the perceived conflict between faith and science is a stumbling block for many, Christians who embody a thoughtful, informed, and integrative approach can be powerful witnesses. They can demonstrate that faith is not about closing one's mind to knowledge but is an invitation to explore the depth and breadth of truth with an open heart and mind.

In conclusion, the discussion around evolution and Christian doctrine is not merely an intellectual exercise; it is a spiritual journey toward a more profound understanding of our faith and the world. As we embark on this journey, let us do so with humility, curiosity, and a relentless pursuit of truth, guided by the belief that in seeking to understand God's creation more deeply, we come to know the Creator more intimately. May this exploration deepen our faith, broaden our perspectives, and inspire us to live out our calling as stewards of this magnificent and sacred reality we call creation.

Chapter 10:
The Power of Testimony - Personal
Experiences and Witness

Moving beyond the tangible evidence and the debates that engage the intellect, we arrive at a domain that resonates with the heart—the realm of testimony and personal experience. The Christian faith, rich in historical claims and philosophical arguments, also thrives on the profound and often transformative stories of individuals whose lives speak volumes of a reality beyond what can be seen or measured. Within these narratives lies the undeniable power of changed lives, a testament not just to belief, but to lived experience. The skeptic may question a text's historicity or the philosopher debate a concept's validity, but the personal journey of faith, marked by radical transformation and newfound purpose, stands as a beacon of light in a realm often clouded by doubt. It is in the retelling of these journeys, from despair to hope, from aimlessness to a sense of divine mission, that the Christian message finds one of its most compelling forms of witness. As we explore the significance and implications of these stories, we delve into the role of personal transformation, not as anecdotal evidence to be dismissed, but as a powerful form of testimony to the truth and impact of the Christian faith. Each story, unique in its contours, contributes to the larger narrative of a faith that has the power to change lives, to uplift the downtrodden, and to instill a purpose that transcends the ordinary—underscoring the profound belief that at the heart of Christianity lies the capacity for personal and communal transformation that echoes through generations.

The Role of Personal Transformation

In the fabric of Christian testimony, personal transformation stands as a vivid thread weaving through the stories of countless believers, offering a compelling witness to the power of faith. This transformation is not merely an internal renovation but represents a profound metamorphosis that echoes into families, communities, and beyond. At its core, personal transformation within a Christian context transcends the boundaries of mere nalysent modification; it is an about-face turn inspired by an encounter with the divine, a heartfelt response to the inexplicable love and grace emanating from the crucified and risen Christ. As believers experience this radical change, their lives become a beacon of hope and evidence of a reality transformed through Christ. This transformation, marked by renewed perspectives, values, and purposes, furnishes not only a powerful rebuttal to the skeptics' doubts but also serves as a persuasive invitation to those on the fringes of faith. It underscores the notion that Christianity is not simply a set of doctrines to assent to but a dynamic, life-altering journey with the living God. The authenticity and depth of such personal transformations fortify the Christian witness, underlining the veracity of the Gospel message and its capacity to change lives profoundly and permanently.

Conversion Stories: Significance and Implications

The chapters leading up to this moment have meticulously laid the foundation, introducing us to the role and impact of Christianity on individual lives and cultures, arguing the reliability of scripture, the rationality of miracles, and the profound depth of Christian ethics and morality. Now, we pivot towards the personal, the intimate experiences that serve as a confluence of the intellectual and the spiritual: conversion stories.

At the heart of every conversion story is a journey, not just a transition of belief but a transformation of the soul. These narratives are not merely accounts of change; they are testament to the power of faith to renovate the most inner chambers of the human heart. In engaging with conversion stories, we do not simply learn about the end result of faith, but we uncover the pathways through which many have navigated the complexities of doubt, struggle, and ultimately, belief.

Conversion stories resonate because they are relatable. They speak to the universal quest for meaning, purpose, and truth that is inherent in the human experience. Whether one is steadfast in their faith or wandering in the wilderness of nalysent, there's an undeniable allure in the stories of those who have crossed the Rubicon of doubt to embrace faith wholeheartedly. It is this relatability that makes these stories potent tools in the hands of believers, providing not just evidence of the transformative power of belief but also serving as a beacon for those still on their journey.

However, the significance of conversion stories extends beyond their inspirational value. They are a vital component of Christian apologetics. In a world that often demands empirical evidence for belief, personal testimonies offer a different kind of proof, one that is experiential and existential. While they do not replace the need for historical, philosophical, or scientific engagement with the tenets of Christianity, they complement these discussions with living examples of the faith in action.

When we examine the implications of conversion stories, we see that they are a powerful antidote to the sterility of purely intellectual debates about faith. They infuse the dialogue with warmth and humanity, reminding us that at the center of all theological discourse are real people, with real experiences of transformation and renewal.

This personal dimension can often reach places that logical arguments alone cannot, touching hearts in ways that reason can only aspire to.

For skeptics and seekers, conversion stories offer a glimpse into the potential for change, suggesting that if such transformations are possible for others, they might be possible for them too. They represent not just proof of Christian beliefs but an invitation to explore those beliefs further, to see them not just as abstract propositions but as pathways to personal and spiritual nalysent.

Furthermore, conversion stories are not monolithic; they reflect a kaleidoscope of experiences, backgrounds, and cultures. This diversity underscores the universal appeal of Christianity, suggesting that it speaks to a multitude of human needs and desires, transcending geographical, cultural, and linguistic barriers. It is a vivid demonstration of Christianity's claim to offer not just a regional or cultural faith, but a universal path to truth.

Yet, while the impact of conversion stories is profound, it is essential for Christians to approach these narratives with sensitivity and respect. Each story is deeply personal, and while they may serve as powerful examples of the faith, they should never be reduced to mere tools for proselytization. Instead, they should be shared in a spirit of humility and with a recognition of the courage it often takes for individuals to make such profound changes in their lives.

In sharing conversion stories, believers must also be mindful of the diverse contexts in which they are received. What inspires one heart may not move another, and what strengthens one's faith might challenge or even alienate another. It is in this space of diversity and difference that the true art of Christian apologetics flourishes: the ability to engage thoughtfully and respectfully with a wide range of experiences and perspectives.

Moreover, conversion stories highlight the ongoing journey of faith. Rarely are these narratives about a sudden, isolated epiphany; more often, they are about a process, a series of encounters, questions, and moments of clarity that gradually lead someone home to faith. They remind us that faith itself is not a static achievement but a dynamic, evolving relationship with the Divine.

This dynamic nature of faith reinforces the idea that conversion is not simply a one-time event but the beginning of a lifelong journey. It underscores the significance of community, fellowship, and ongoing spiritual growth. As such, conversion stories can serve as milestones, commemorating where one has come from while also looking forward to where one is called to go.

In essence, conversion stories are a celebration of grace. They bear witness to the action of God in individual lives, how He meets people where they are, and lovingly guides them towards Himself. It is here, in these personal histories, that the abstract concepts of grace, forgiveness, and redemption become tangible, painted in the vivid colors of lived experience.

Ultimately, the significance and implications of conversion stories within Christianity cannot be overstated. They are both evidence of and invitation to a life transformed by faith. They challenge, inspire, and encourage, standing as monuments to the power of belief. For believers, they are a source of strength and reassurance; for seekers, a light leading towards hope and transformation.

In closing, whether one is a believer seeking to deepen their faith or a seeker on the edge of belief, conversion stories stand as a testament to the life-changing power of faith. They are a reminder that within the heart of Christianity is the promise of renewal, transformation, and the infinite possibilities that await on the journey of faith.

Analyzing Personal Testimony as Evidence

In our journey through understanding and defending Christian beliefs, we come upon the powerful, often transformative realm of personal testimony. Within the context of Christianity, personal testimony holds a significant place, acting as both a beacon of personal change and evidence of the divine at work in people's lives. This chapter aims to explore the depth and authenticity of personal testimony and how it stands as evidence within Christian apologetics.

At the outset, it's essential to acknowledge that the power of personal testimony cannot be underestimated. These narratives often contain raw, emotional accounts of lives transformed, addictions conquered, and hope restored. They speak to the heart in ways that intellectual arguments sometimes cannot. However, when evaluating personal testimony as evidence for the truth of Christianity, one must proceed with both openness and discernment.

First, consider the historical relevance of testimony. The Christian faith itself was spread and has been sustained through centuries by the personal testimonies of its believers. From the apostles' eyewitness accounts of Jesus' life, death, and resurrection to contemporary stories of transformed lives, personal testimony is deeply woven into the fabric of Christian experience and tradition.

Yet, when presented as evidence, personal testimony invites scrutiny. Skeptics may argue that personal experiences are subjective, influenced by a person's psychological state, cultural background, or even wishful thinking. While it's true that personal experiences are subjective, dismissing them entirely overlooks the profound, often undeniable changes in a person's life that defy simple psychological explanations.

For evidence to be credible, it doesn't necessarily have to be quantifiable or reproducible in a lab. In the court of law, eyewitness testimony, under the right conditions, is considered powerful evidence. Similarly, the transformative effects observed in the lives of believers can be seen as compelling evidence of the truth and power of Christian claims.

Analysis of personal testimony as evidence also requires a look into consistency. Across time and cultures, countless individuals from vastly different backgrounds report remarkably similar experiences of transformation when they encounter the Christian message. This universality suggests a common source of truth, one that transcends individual subjective experiences.

Moreover, the authenticity of personal testimony can often be corroborated by external changes. When a person's life undergoes a radical transformation for the better—overcoming addictions, restoring relationships, adopting a more selfless lifestyle—these are observable facts. The outward evidence of internal transformation lends credibility to personal testimony.

It's also worth considering the cost of such testimonies. Throughout history, many have shared their personal experiences with Christianity at great personal risk, even facing persecution or death. The willingness to suffer for one's faith adds a profound level of authenticity to personal testimonies.

However, one must also be cautious. Not all claims made in personal testimonies can be taken at face value without discernment. It's important to seek consistency, not just within Christianity but with the reality we observe around us. A testimony that claims something contrary to clear evidential truth requires careful scrutiny.

The role of personal testimony in apologetics does not stand in isolation but is most effective when combined with other forms of evidence. It complements historical, philosophical, and scientific arguments, enriching the tapestry of evidence that supports Christian truth claims.

In engaging with skeptics and seekers, the personal aspect should not be overlooked. While arguments and debates can appeal to the intellect, personal stories touch the heart. They provide a concrete, relatable example of how abstract concepts like grace, forgiveness, and transformation are lived out in the real world.

For those exploring or challenging the Christian faith, consider not just the stories themselves but the lives behind them. Look for the fruits of transformation, for as the Christian scripture says, "by their fruits, you will know them." Investigate the authenticity, consistency, and implications of these stories.

Faith, after all, is not without evidence, and personal testimony stands as a profound, vibrant part of that evidence. It invites listeners into a story bigger than themselves, offering a glimpse of the divine at work in the messiness of human life. It stands as a testament not just to a set of beliefs, but to a living, dynamic relationship with the divine that transforms lives.

In conclusion, when we nalyse personal testimony as evidence within Christian apologetics, we are reminded of the power of story, the authenticity of transformed lives, and the personal nature of faith. It challenges us to look beyond mere facts and figures and consider the profound impact of the Christian message on individual lives. In doing so, we find compelling evidence of the truth and power of the Christian faith, an evidence that speaks to both the heart and mind.

In engaging with the world as Christians, let us remember the value of our own stories and the stories of those around us. For in every testimony, there is a potential for profound impact—a beacon of hope, a call to faith, and a witness to the transformative power of God's love. Let us hold these testimonies as precious evidence, sharing them with both humility and boldness as we continue the divine dialogue in a world that is in desperate need of a message of hope and transformation.

Chapter 11:
Living Apologetics – The Role of the
Christian in Public Discourse

In the vibrant mosaic of public discourse, the voice of the Christian, equipped with the knowledge and wisdom of apologetics, plays a critical role that extends far beyond the confines of church walls. It is here, in the bustling fora of societal dialogue, that the Christian is called not merely to participate but to radiate a presence of understanding, compassion, and unwavering conviction. This chapter delves into the essence of living apologetics, an art that intertwines the threads of faith into the fabric of everyday conversations, showcasing that apologetics is not confined to scholarly debate but is a lived experience, a testament to the transformative power of faith. Engaging with respect and grace becomes not just a method, but a mission; for in the gentle art of conversation, one discovers the opportunity to plant seeds of truth in the most fertile soil of human hearts. The challenge before us is monumental yet invigorating: to navigate the treacherous waters of skepticism and relativism, armed with the twin oars of reason and love. This chapter aims to equip believers with the tools to navigate these conversations with grace, understanding that our call to apologetics is not a call to win arguments, but to win souls, guiding them towards the light of truth with patience, humility, and an unwavering commitment to the Gospel message. Through embodying the principles of apologetics in our daily interactions, we illuminate the path for others, making the Christian faith a living, breathing reality that challenges, uplifts, and inspires.

Apologetics in Everyday Conversations

In the intricate dance of life, where ideas and beliefs cross-paths, apologetics finds its most vibrant stage not in the lecture halls or pulpit but in the ordinary moments of everyday conversations. It's in the sharing of a meal, the casual exchanges at work, or the late-night talks where the essence of living out apologetics truly unfolds. For the Christian committed to engaging thoughtfully with the world, these interactions are not mere coincidences but divinely appointed opportunities to reflect Christ's love and truth.

A personal approach to apologetics requires a genuine commitment to understanding the individual before you. Listen intently, not solely for the opening to present a counter-argument, but to truly grasp where the other person is coming from. Their doubts, their objections, and their questions often stem from deeper quests for truth, meaning, and hope. Your willingness to walk alongside them in their journey can transform what begins as a debate into a meaningful dialogue.

The art of apologetics in everyday interactions leans heavily on a spirit of humility and grace. Delve into discussions with the understanding that we ourselves are on a journey, continuously learning and growing. When we adopt a posture of humility, acknowledging that we don't have all the answers, our conversations become less about winning an argument and more about mutual exploration of profound truths.

Do not shy away from difficult questions. The complexities of faith and the pressing doubts of our age demand thoughtful consideration. When faced with questions you can't answer, see it not as a defeat, but as an opportunity to delve deeper into the mysteries of faith together. It's a journey you embark on with the person, showing them that their questions and doubts do not intimidate your faith but invigorate it.

Grace underpins every successful conversation. Responding to skepticism and challenges with gentleness and respect disarms hostility and opens doors for meaningful discourse. Remember, it's not just what we say but how we say it that leaves a lasting impact. Our goal isn't to prove ourselves right but to show the transforming love and truth of Christ.

Incorporate your personal testimony into your conversations judiciously. Your story of faith, with all its triumphs and trials, can be a powerful witness to the reality of God's work in your life. However, balance is crucial. Share your story in a way that connects with the other person's experiences and emotional world, making it relevant and compelling to them.

Practical wisdom is indispensable in navigating these conversations. Not every moment is the right time for a theological discussion, and discernment is key to recognizing when to speak and when to listen. Sometimes, the most profound form of apologetics is simply being a faithful, loving presence in someone's life, embodying the virtues of Christ.

Know the core truths of your faith deeply. Grounding in Scripture and the historical tenets of Christianity equip you to engage with both confidence and depth. This solid foundation not only informs your understanding but also illuminates your conversation, providing clear reference points for discussion.

Embrace the questions and allow them to challenge and refine your faith. Every query, every objection invites us to delve deeper into our beliefs, to question, and to grow. This process not only strengthens our own faith but also equips us to engage more meaningfully with others.

Diversify your understanding and appreciation of Christian thought. Exploring different theological perspectives within Christianity enriches your understanding and allows you to engage with a broader audience. This familiarity enables you to bridge gaps and find common ground in shared values and beliefs.

Be patient and persistent. Transformative conversations rarely happen in a single sitting. They unfold over time, through layers of dialogue, demonstrating the persistent love and grace of God. Your steadfastness in the face of doubt and opposition can itself be a powerful testimony to the truth and relevance of your faith.

Ultimately, apologetics in everyday conversations is about embodying the love, grace, and truth of the gospel. It's about seeing each interaction as a divine appointment to reflect Christ's light into the lives of those around us. It transcends mere argumentation, reaching into the very essence of what it means to live out our faith authentically and invitingly in the world.

As we embark on this journey of integrating apologetics into our everyday interactions, let us do so with hearts open to learning and spirits attuned to the guiding whisper of the Holy Spirit. Let our words be seasoned with grace, our lives be testimonies of love, and our hearts always ready to give an answer for the hope that we have. But above all, let us do this with gentleness and respect, knowing that our ultimate aim is not to win arguments but to win hearts for Christ.

In this sacred endeavor, we are mere vessels, channels of God's grace and truth. Let us, therefore, walk in humility, empowered by the Spirit, engaging the world not as adversaries but as ambassadors of hope. In every conversation, in every question, in every challenge, may we reflect the love of Christ, demonstrating that faith is not a distant ideal but a living reality, vibrantly relevant in the fabric of everyday life.

Embrace apologetics as an integral aspect of your spiritual journey, an opportunity to live out the transformative power of the gospel in real and meaningful ways. As you do, remember that it's in those small, seemingly mundane interactions that the greatest opportunities for witness often lie. Seize them with courage and love, for in this calling, you become a beacon of hope, a living apologetic, proof of God's enduring presence in the world.

Engaging with Respect and Grace

As we delve into the nuanced field of Christian apologetics, especially within the vast expanse of public discourse, an imperative approach emerges—one of engaging with both respect and grace. This dual approach is not merely a suggestion; it is the bedrock on which effective, meaningful conversations are built. Encountering a spectrum of beliefs, perspectives, and, at times, staunch criticisms, requires a disposition that embodies the very core of Christ-like dialogues.

Respect, in this context, transcends mere politeness. It's about earnestly valuing the other person's viewpoint, understanding their background, and recognizing their dignity as individuals. When we engage with respect, we're not conceding our beliefs; instead, we're creating a space where open, honest exchange can flourish. This allows for a dialogue that doesn't aim to overpower but to understand and to be understood.

Grace, on the other hand, is about extending kindness, patience, and forgiveness in conversations, especially when they veer into contentious terrains. It's about maintaining a posture of love, even when faced with hostility. Engaging with grace means our words are seasoned with compassion, reflecting the heart of the Gospel message.

It's acknowledging that our ultimate goal is not to win an argument but to win a person over to Christ's love.

These approaches are critical when navigating complex issues within public discourse. Topics like moral relativism, the existence of suffering, and the historicity of Jesus demand more than just intellectual readiness; they require an emotional and spiritual sensitivity that respects and values the individual on the other side of the conversation.

A practical step in applying respect is to actively listen. This involves more than just waiting for your turn to speak. It's about genuinely trying to understand where the other person is coming from, asking clarifying questions, and even repeating back what you've heard to ensure comprehension. This practice not only demonstrates respect but often softens hearts and opens doors to more effective communication.

Simultaneously, employing grace might mean choosing your battles wisely. Not every point of contention needs to be addressed in the moment. Sometimes, extending grace means prioritizing the relationship over the dispute, allowing for future opportunities to share your perspective. It's in these moments of restraint that we often display the strength of our character and the depth of our faith.

Moreover, engaging with respect and grace doesn't imply avoiding tough questions or shying away from proclaiming truth. On the contrary, it's about presenting the Christian worldview with such empathy and understanding that the truth becomes irresistible. It's about making the Gospel appealing not just through our arguments but through the way we argue.

One of the most profound ways to embody respect and grace is through our personal testimony. Sharing how Christ has transformed our lives can be a powerful tool in apologetics. It's a narrative that's uniquely ours, and when shared authentically, it can break down walls and touch hearts in ways that intellectual arguments might not.

In addition, incorporating prayer into our engagements is paramount. Praying for wisdom, guidance, and for the hearts of those we're engaging with aligns our efforts with God's will. It's a reminder that ultimately, it's not our eloquence or knowledge that changes hearts, but the Holy Spirit's work through our willingness to serve as vessels.

However, it's also important to recognize and accept our limitations. There will be conversations that don't go the way we hope, and people whose hearts remain hardened. In these moments, engaging with respect and grace means knowing when to step back, entrusting the individual into God's capable hands, while keeping the door open for future dialogue.

Furthermore, this approach requires humility—a recognition that we don't have all the answers and that we, too, are on a journey of understanding and growth. It's a posture that invites others into a shared exploration of truth, rather than positioning ourselves as having reached the pinnacle of knowledge.

As Christians, we're called to be ambassadors for Christ, a role that demands a delicate balance of truth and love, conviction and compassion. Engaging with respect and grace is not just about being nice; it's about reflecting the character of Jesus in every interaction. It's about ensuring that our message is not only heard but truly received.

Let us take up this challenge with a sense of purpose and dedication, knowing that our role in the public discourse is not just to defend a set of beliefs, but to demonstrate through our words and actions, the transformative power of living a life anchored in Christ. This is the essence of living apologetics: to engage not just with arguments, but with hearts, with respect, and with grace.

As we forge ahead, may we continuously seek to refine our approach, remembering that each conversation is an opportunity to plant seeds of faith, hope, and love. May we be mindful that in every encounter, we're not only addressing minds but engaging souls, shaping not just perceptions, but potentially, eternities. Let this be the passion that drives us and the vision that guides our every word and action in the public square.

Chapter 12:
End Times and Prophecy - Interpreting Apocalyptic Literature

In an ever-evolving world that often seems shrouded in mystery and marred by uncertainty, the Christian narrative of the end times and prophecy serves as a lighthouse for souls adrift in a sea of skepticism. This chapter delves into the fascinating realm of apocalyptic literature, a genre that, through its vivid imagery and symbolic language, invites us to view the ultimate unfolding of human history through a lens tinted with hope, justice, and divine sovereignty. As we embark on this journey of interpretation, it's crucial to understand these texts not merely as predictors of doom but as profound reflections on the human condition, offering guidance for living purposefully in the present. By exploring different viewpoints on the end times and analyzing prophecy through both predictive and poetic lenses, we embark on an enlightening quest. This quest unearths the robustness of Christian thought, revealing an intellectual treasure trove capable of equipping believers to defend their faith with confidence while engaging thoughtfully with seekers and skeptics alike. Thus, as we navigate these apocalyptic passages, let us be inspired to anchor our lives in the bedrock of faith, propelled by the promise of redemption and the unwavering hope for a world remade in divine perfection.

Different Views on the End Times

The topic of the End Times, or eschatology, within Christian theology has sparked intrigue, debate, and fervent anticipation for centuries. It's a theme that transcends mere theological discussion, touching the hearts and minds of believers and seekers alike, awakening a universal curiosity about the future of humanity and the cosmos. This chapter aims to illuminate the various perspectives Christians hold on the End Times, inviting readers into a deeper understanding that, while diverse, contributes to the rich tapestry of Christian belief.

One prevailing view is known as Premillennialism, which posits that Christ will return before a literal thousand-year reign on Earth. This perspective often emphasizes a period of tribulation, during which believers endure hardship and persecution before the triumphant second coming of Jesus. It's a view marked by expectancy and a literal interpretation of apocalyptic literature, seeing prophetic scriptures as a roadmap to the future events of the End Times.

Contrastingly, Amillennialism offers a different lens through which to interpret these scriptures. Amillennialists view the thousand-year reign of Christ not as a literal future event, but as a symbolic period representing the current reign of Christ in heaven and in the hearts of believers. From this perspective, the End Times are not seen as a future sequence of events but as an ongoing spiritual reality, culminating in the ultimate victory of good over evil.

Postmillennialism introduces yet another viewpoint, suggesting that through the spread of the Christian gospel and the influence of the church, the world will gradually improve, leading into an age of peace and righteousness. This era, often equated with the millennial reign, is believed to precede Christ's return. Thus, postmillennialists maintain an optimistic view of the future, emphasizing the transformative power of the gospel to change the world.

The Historical Premillennialism perspective, akin to traditional Premillennialism, believes in Christ's return before a literal reign on Earth. However, it is distinguished by its emphasis on the historical approach to interpreting scripture, focusing on the early church's expectations and teachings about the End Times.

In the midst of these perspectives, Partial Preterism offers an intriguing standpoint. It asserts that many of the prophecies in the New Testament were fulfilled in the first century, specifically through the destruction of Jerusalem in AD 70. This view sees Biblical apocalyptic language as symbolic, speaking to contemporary events of the early church rather than to future occurrences.

Each of these perspectives stems from a devoted attempt to understand and interpret one of the Bible's most complex and allegorical components. It's important to approach this exploration with humility, recognizing that our finite minds may struggle to fully grasp the infinite plans of the Divine.

Examining these different views encourages a spirit of unity rather than division. It's a reminder that our hope is not found in perfectly aligning with one eschatological viewpoint but in the shared anticipation of Christ's ultimate victory and the restoration of all things. This binds believers together in a common hope that transcends theological differences.

The discussion of End Times should not lead to fear or anxiety but should inspire hope and a deeper commitment to live out our faith today. Understanding the various perspectives enriches our spiritual journey, inviting us to live with anticipation and to engage actively in God's work in the world, no matter our stance on eschatology.

Engaging with different views on the End Times also strengthens our apologetic foundations. It equips us to converse intelligently and graciously with skeptics and seekers, providing reasoned responses and demonstrating the breadth of thought within Christian eschatology.

As we navigate through the complexities of these viewpoints, let's embrace the mystery with faith, recognizing that there are elements of God's plan that may remain beyond our comprehension until they unfold. This humble admission is not a weakness but a testament to the depth and mystery of our faith.

In this exploration, it's crucial to remember that our unity in Christ surpasses any eschatological differences. The core of our faith, grounded in the life, death, and resurrection of Jesus Christ, forms the foundation upon which we can respectfully engage in discussions about the End Times.

Let the exploration of these diverse views on the End Times be a journey that deepens your faith, broadens your understanding, and strengthens your ability to engage in meaningful conversations about the Christian hope for the future. It's an invitation to marvel at the vastness of God's plan for humanity and to find our place within the story He is unfolding.

Finally, as we consider these different perspectives, let's do so with the knowledge that our ultimate hope is not in fully comprehending every detail of the End Times but in trusting the One who holds the future. Our faith is rooted not in a specific eschatological viewpoint but in a Person—Jesus Christ, whose love and promises are sure, regardless of how the last chapters of history unfold.

In conclusion, the diversity of thought within Christian eschatology enriches our collective understanding and anticipation of the future. It's an area of theology that invites deep study, prayerful reflection, and vibrant discussion—all of which can draw us closer to God and to each other as we navigate the complexities of faith with an open heart and mind. Let us approach these conversations with grace, wisdom, and a spirit of unity that reflects the love and hope we have in Christ.

Prophecy as Apologetic: Predictive Vs. Poetic

Embarking on a journey through the tapestry of prophecy within Christian apologetics, we encounter a compelling narrative that serves not just as a historical or future roadmap but as a dynamic expression of faith. Prophecy in the biblical sense often straddles the realms of the predictive and the poetic—an interplay that is both intriguing and enlightening. The understanding of this dual nature can significantly bolster the Christian's ability to engage in thoughtful dialogue about the essence of hope and foreknowledge encapsulated in scripture.

At the heart of predictive prophecy lies the assertion that certain events were foretold by biblical prophets with astonishing accuracy. These prophecies, often cited by apologists, serve to affirm the divine inspiration of scripture. They are seen as concrete evidence that God, operating outside of time, communicated specific details about future events, particularly concerning the life of Jesus, the spread of the Gospel, and the end times.

However, to view prophecy solely through the lens of prediction is to miss the breadth of its richness and depth. Biblical prophecy also embodies a poetic dimension, where metaphor, symbolism, and allegory are employed extensively. This poetic aspect invites the reader into a deeper engagement with the text, requiring contemplation and reflection to unveil the layers of meaning beneath the surface. It is here, in the poetic, that prophecy stirs the soul, sparks the imagination, and speaks to the human condition in a profoundly personal way.

Understanding prophecy as both predictive and poetic allows for a more nuanced and comprehensive approach to apologetics. It enables believers to present a case for Christianity that is not only grounded in factual evidences but also resonates with the emotional and spiritual experiences of the individual. This dual perspective not only fortifies faith but also enriches the dialogue with skeptics and seekers by appealing to both reason and empathy.

One of the challenges in interpreting prophetic literature is navigating the tension between these two aspects. Historical fulfillment of prophecy is subject to scrutiny and debate, often requiring a meticulous examination of historical records and contextual analysis. Critics may argue that predictions are too vague or that their fulfillment is contrived or coincidental. In response, apologists must carefully weigh the evidence, considering the specificity, timing, and context of each prophecy and its corresponding fulfillment.

Conversely, the poetic nature of prophecy, while less susceptible to empirical validation, offers a fertile ground for spiritual and existential exploration. The symbols and metaphors found in biblical prophecy speak to universal themes—justice, redemption, suffering, and renewal—that transcend time and culture. Engaging with the poetic allows for a dynamic interpretation of prophecy that can address the needs and challenges of every generation.

In bridging the gap between the predictive and the poetic, it is vital to maintain a balance that honors both the intellectual integrity and the spiritual vitality of Christian faith. Apologists are tasked with the delicate endeavor of presenting evidence for predictive prophecy without neglecting the transformative power of its poetic counterpart. This balanced approach not only strengthens the apologetic endeavor but also fosters a faith that is both intellectually robust and deeply personal.

Furthermore, the interplay between predictive and poetic prophecy serves as a testament to the multifaceted nature of divine revelation. It demonstrates that God's communication with humanity is not limited to mere foretelling of events but encompasses a rich tapestry of expressions designed to engage the whole person—mind, heart, and spirit.

As we delve deeper into the study of prophecy within the apologetic realm, it becomes apparent that prophecy is not merely a tool for prediction but a means of revelation. It reveals the heart of God, His plans for humanity, and His involvement in the course of human history. Prophecy, therefore, is an invitation to trust in the faithfulness of God, who not only knows the future but is also intimately involved in the journey of His people.

In engaging with skeptics and seekers, the dual aspect of prophecy as both predictive and poetic provides a rich ground for dialogue. It allows for conversations that not only address the intellect but also connect with the existential questions and spiritual longings of every human heart. By embracing both perspectives, believers can present a more holistic and compelling case for the Christian faith—one that validates the reliability of scripture and testifies to the transformative power of God's word.

Ultimately, the exploration of prophecy as apologetic, with its blend of predictive and poetic elements, challenges us to expand our understanding of divine revelation. It calls us to approach scripture with both a critical mind and an open heart, recognizing that prophecy serves as a bridge between heaven and earth, between the divine and the human. In this sacred space of encounter, we find not only evidences for faith but also invitations to experience the profound mystery and beauty of a God who speaks to us across time.

As we continue this journey, let us hold fast to the conviction that prophecy, in all its complexity and mystery, is a gift—an apologetic that not only defends but also declares the glory of God. It is a beacon that guides us through the uncertainties of life, pointing us toward a future filled with hope and anchored in the promise of eternal redemption. In embracing both the predictive and poetic aspects of prophecy, we find ourselves equipped to navigate the challenges of apologetics with grace, wisdom, and confidence.

In conclusion, prophecy stands as a cornerstone of Christian apologetics, offering a unique lens through which to view the veracity and vitality of the Christian faith. By engaging with both its predictive and poetic dimensions, we deepen our understanding, enrich our faith, and strengthen our witness to a world in search of hope and truth. Let us, therefore, embrace the study of prophecy with a spirit of humility and expectation, ever mindful of the profound ways in which God reveals Himself to us through His word.

Book review request

In our journey through understanding the nuanced interpretations of apocalyptic literature within "End Times and Prophecy," we invite you to further enrich this exploration by sharing your insights or reviews for this book online. Thank you.

Chapter 13:
Continuing the Divine Dialogue - A Call to Informed Faith

A s we turn the final pages of this exploration into the Christian faith and its rational, historical, and spiritual underpinnings, we arrive at a vital juncture. This moment is not an end but a commencement—the beginning of a lifelong journey of understanding, engagement, and growth. The landscape of faith, after all, is not static. It shifts and evolves, beckoning us to continue our pursuit of knowledge and wisdom within the divine dialogue.

Throughout this discourse, we have traversed the realms of history, science, philosophy, and personal experience. We've dissected and delved deeply into the complexities and simplicities that frame Christian apologetics. Yet, the essence of our journey underscores a much broader call—a call to informed faith, one that challenges, nurtures, and expands our spiritual horizons.

Informed faith is not passive. It engages with the world, eagerly wrestling with questions and challenges, and, in doing so, it becomes more resilient and nuanced. This journey fosters a robust framework for understanding, enabling believers to navigate the often-turbulent waters of skepticism and doubt with grace and confidence.

Embracing informed faith also means rejecting the false dichotomy between faith and reason. As we've explored, these realms are not mutually exclusive but deeply intertwined. The Christian tradition, with its rich intellectual heritage, offers profound insights into the harmony of faith and reason, revealing a faith that is as logical as it is spiritual.

Our exploration has further revealed that the historical and philosophical foundations of Christianity are not merely academic exercises but are deeply impactful for personal faith. Understanding the historical Jesus, the reliability of scripture, and the rationality of miracles adds dimension and strength to our belief, enriching our spiritual lives and our engagement with the world around us.

Moreover, we've seen that Christianity does not exist in isolation. It interacts dynamically with science, other religions, and contemporary ethical questions, inviting Christians to engage in thoughtful dialogue and respectful debate. Through such engagement, we not only defend but also deepen our faith, discovering new perspectives and insights that enrich our understanding.

Significantly, this journey towards informed faith is not solitary. It unfolds within the context of community—among fellow seekers and believers, each with their unique insights, questions, and experiences. By sharing our journeys, engaging in open dialogue, and offering mutual support, we strengthen not only our faith but also the larger body of Christ.

Living apologetics is another critical aspect of continuing the divine dialogue. It's about embodying the principles and truths we espouse, demonstrating the transformative power of faith through our lives. This authentic witness is perhaps the most persuasive form of apologetics, speaking deeply to the hearts of those around us.

As we move forward, it's crucial to remember that doubt and questioning are not antithetical to faith but are, in many ways, expressions of it. They push us to seek deeper understanding, to grapple with difficult issues, and ultimately, to grow in confidence and conviction. Informed faith, therefore, is one that embraces questions as part of the divine dialogue.

Yet, we must also be mindful of the attitudes with which we approach these discussions. Humility, respect, and grace are indispensable. In every conversation, whether with skeptics or fellow believers, our goal is not victory but understanding—seeking not to conquer but to connect, and in doing so, reflecting the love and wisdom of Christ.

This journey toward informed faith is, in essence, a divine calling. It's an invitation to engage more deeply with the truths of Christianity, to explore and wrestle with its claims, and to emerge with a faith that is not only intellectually satisfying but also deeply transformative.

As we continue this divine dialogue, let's do so with a sense of wonder and openness, always ready to learn, to grow, and to be surprised. The path of informed faith is a journey of discovery, rich with insights and revelations that deepen our understanding of God, the world, and ourselves.

In closing, the call to informed faith is not just about defending Christianity against skepticism or understanding its historical and philosophical underpinnings. It's about embracing a journey that transforms us, equipping us to navigate life's questions and challenges with faith that is reasoned, vibrant, and deeply grounded in love.

So, let us move forward with courage and conviction, informed by the rich legacy of Christian thought, and inspired by the transformative power of faith. Let us continue the divine dialogue with hearts and minds open, ready to experience the depth and breadth of a faith that truly informs, transforms, and transcends.

In the end, the journey of faith is an ongoing dialogue—a divine dialogue. It's an invitation to engage with the living God, to ask, seek, and knock with a heart that is eager for truth. And as we respond to this call, we find not just answers but a deeper relationship with the One who calls us each by name. This is the essence of informed faith, and this is our call to continue the divine dialogue.

Appendix A:
Appendix

In our journey through the layers and questions of Christian faith, it's important to recognize that the path does not end with the final page of this book. Rather, it's a vibrant, ongoing exploration that beckons each of us to delve deeper, seek further, and engage more profoundly with our beliefs and the world around us. To aid in this continuous quest, Appendix A offers a trove of resources designed to illuminate, challenge, and enrich your understanding.

A. Recommended Resources for Further Study

The ocean of knowledge and wisdom is vast, and navigating its boundless expanse can be both exhilarating and overwhelming. To guide your voyage, a carefully curated selection of books, articles, websites, and podcasts are recommended. Whether you're seeking to strengthen your grasp of biblical history, deepen your philosophical understanding, or explore the intersection of science and faith, these resources are stepping stones to broader horizons. They serve not only as tools for personal edification but also as bridges for engaging with others on matters of faith and reason.

B. Addressing Common Misconceptions About Christianity

In the pursuit of truth, it's crucial to clear the fog that often enshrouds reality. This section aims to dispel prevalent myths and misconceptions about Christianity, providing clear, concise answers rooted in scholarship and reason. From addressing the supposed conflict between faith and science to clarifying misunderstood doctrines, this resource equips you to navigate conversations with confidence and grace.

C. Practices and Exercises for Effective Apologetics

Apologetics isn't merely an academic discipline; it's a lived practice that extends into every interaction and thought. This section introduces practical, actionable exercises designed to hone your ability to communicate your faith persuasively and empathetically. From refining your understanding of key arguments to developing empathy for those with differing beliefs, these exercises are crafted to strengthen both intellect and character.

As you forge ahead, let your heart and mind be open to the transformative power of inquiry and reflection. The journey of faith is not one of solitary confinement to the echos of our own thoughts, but a communal voyage rich with dialogue, discovery, and growth. May the resources and guidance provided in Appendix A be lamps to your feet and lights to your path, as you navigate the captivating landscape of Christian thought and life.

A. Recommended Resources for Further Study

In our journey to understanding and defending the Christian faith, it's crucial to equip ourselves with a robust arsenal of resources. The path to wise and informed faith is both an adventure and a challenge, a call to delve deeper into the mysteries of our beliefs, and engage thoughtfully with the world around us. As we conclude this narrative, let's venture into a curated selection of resources designed to broaden your horizon and sharpen your insights into Christianity.

First and foremost, a thorough study of the Bible is indispensable. It's not just about reading the Scriptures, but engaging with them, questioning them, and seeking to understand their contexts and teachings. To aid in this endeavor, "The ESV Study Bible" comes highly recommended. It offers extensive notes, historical backgrounds, and explanations to help illuminate the biblical text in a profound way.

For those intrigued by the historical underpinnings of the Christian faith, "The Case for Christ" by Lee Strobel is a fascinating read. As a former investigative journalist, Strobel meticulously examines the historical evidence for Jesus, making a compelling case for the reliability of the New Testament documentation and the reality of Christ's resurrection.

Delving into the realm of philosophy and apologetics, "Mere Christianity" by C.S. Lewis is a timeless classic that eloquently articulates the logical underpinnings of faith. Lewis's ability to distill complex theological concepts into accessible prose makes this book a must-read for both believers and skeptics alike.

In the face of doubts surrounding the coexistence of science and faith, "The Language of God" by Francis S. Collins offers a refreshing perspective. As the leader of the Human Genome Project, Collins shares his journey from atheism to Christianity, arguing that belief in science and faith in God are not only compatible but complementary.

For those wrestling with the problem of evil and suffering, "The Problem of Pain" by C.S. Lewis provides thought-provoking insights into why a loving, omnipotent God allows pain. Lewis navigates this complex issue with grace, offering comfort and understanding to his readers.

On the frontlines of interfaith dialogue, "Jesus Among Other Gods" by Ravi Zacharias eloquently argues for the uniqueness of Jesus Christ among the world's religions. Zacharias's respectful yet uncompromising approach encourages meaningful conversations about faith.

Examining the reliability of scripture, "The New Testament Documents: Are They Reliable?" by F.F. Bruce is an excellent resource. Bruce, a respected biblical scholar, presents a compelling argument for the historical trustworthiness of the New Testament writings.

Those seeking to understand Christian ethics in today's world will find "Moral Choices: An Introduction to Ethics" by Scott B. Rae invaluable. Rae addresses a multitude of ethical dilemmas from a biblical perspective, offering guidance on navigating moral complexities.

"The Reason for God: Belief in an Age of Skepticism" by Timothy Keller engages skeptics and seekers with logical, thoughtful defenses of the Christian faith. Keller's approachable yet scholarly style makes this book a powerful tool for understanding and articulating the reasons for our beliefs.

On the topic of creation and evolution, "The Language of Science and Faith: Straight Answers to Genuine Questions" by Karl W. Giberson and Francis S. Collins bridges the gap between scientific discovery and biblical interpretation. Their dialogue offers clarity and reassurance for those troubled by the perceived conflict between science and scripture.

For a deeper dive into Christian doctrine, "Systematic Theology: An Introduction to Biblical Doctrine" by Wayne Grudem is an extensive work that covers a wide range of theological topics. Grudem's clear and engaging writing makes profound theological concepts accessible to readers at all levels.

In the area of personal testimonies and the transformative power of faith, "The Hiding Place" by Corrie ten Boom stands out. This remarkable story of faith, forgiveness, and survival during the Holocaust inspires readers to see God's hand at work, even in the darkest circumstances.

Confronting the challenges of living out apologetics in the public sphere, "Tactics: A Game Plan for Discussing Your Christian Convictions" by Gregory Koukl equips readers with practical strategies for engaging conversations about faith gracefully and persuasively.

Lastly, as we ponder the end times and prophecy, "Surprised by Hope" by N.T. Wright offers a refreshing look at the Christian hope in resurrection and the transformation of the world. Wright's scholarship invites readers to rethink common misconceptions about heaven and the afterlife.

Let these resources serve as your companions on the journey of faith. As you explore, question, and grow, remember that the quest for understanding is itself a sacred pilgrimage, one that draws us ever closer to the heart of the Divine. Embrace the journey with an open heart and mind, allowing the light of knowledge to guide your steps on the path of truth.

B. Addressing Common Misconceptions About Christianity

In the journey of faith and understanding, misconceptions can act as barriers, obscuring the true essence of what Christianity represents. It's pertinent, then, to dispel these myths, not just for clarity but to foster a deeper, more authentic connection with the divine and with each other. Misconceptions, after all, aren't merely incorrect views; they are missed opportunities for enrichment and dialogue.

One prevalent misconception is that Christianity demands blind faith, sidelining reason and inquiry. This couldn't be farther from the truth. In the rich tapestry of Christian thought, faith and reason are not adversaries but allies. The Christian tradition houses a wealth of philosophers and theologians who have ardently argued that faith is both a matter of the heart and the intellect. It encourages questions, recognizing them as pathways to deeper understanding and stronger conviction.

Another common misunderstanding is the perception of Christianity as a monolith, devoid of diversity. Historically and presently, Christianity is a mosaic, rich with various traditions, interpretations, and practices. From the contemplative practices of Eastern Orthodoxy to the vibrant worship services of Pentecostalism, Christianity encompasses a range of expressions, each contributing unique insights into the breadth of Christian experience and understanding.

Many people also believe that Christianity is incompatible with science, seeing them in constant conflict. Yet, numerous Christians are scientists, and many scientists throughout history have been Christians, viewing their work as a means of exploring and understanding God's creation. The supposed conflict between science and faith often stems from misunderstandings or misrepresentations of either side, rather than an irreconcilable rift.

It's frequently argued that Christianity is fundamentally intolerant, given its claims to truth and exclusivity. However, this overlooks the deep wellspring of love, grace, and forgiveness that lies at the heart of the Christian message. The call to love one's neighbor, including one's enemies, challenges followers of Christ to practice tolerance and compassion, even in the face of disagreement.

The portrayal of Christian ethics as outdated or oppressive is another misconception that merits correction. Christian moral teachings, centered around the virtues of love, honesty, and humility, are not arbitrary rules but paths towards a fulfilling and communal life. They invite individuals to consider not just their desires but the well-being of others, promoting a society founded on mutual respect and care.

There's also a misconception that Christianity dismisses the value of other religions or spiritual paths, presenting itself as the sole repository of truth. While Christianity does make exclusive truth claims, it also recognizes the presence of truth, beauty, and virtue in other faith traditions. Recognizing these elements can become grounds for meaningful dialogue and mutual enrichment, rather than contention.

Some view Christianity as an escape from reality, a crutch for the weak. This misunderstanding ignores the robust Christian tradition of engaging with the world's pain and injustice head-on. Christianity calls its adherents to be agents of change, offering hope and healing. Far from an opiate, it's a source of strength and motivation to confront suffering and work towards a world reflecting divine love and justice.

The belief that Christianity is politically aligned with a single perspective is another distortion. Throughout history, Christians have found their home across the political spectrum, drawing on their faith to advocate for varied visions of justice and the common good. Christianity transcends political affiliation, inviting a critical engagement with all societal structures.

Finally, the notion that Christianity is solely about personal salvation and a ticket to an afterlife reduces its rich narrative to a transaction. While eternal life is a profound aspect of Christian faith, the teachings of Jesus also emphasize the transformation of the here and now — calling for a life lived in love, service, and the pursuit of justice.

Addressing these misconceptions isn't just an exercise in correction but an invitation to dialogue and understanding. It's an opportunity to explore the depths of a faith that has inspired and sustained billions over the millennia.

As we journey together in understanding, may we approach each misconception not as a barrier but as a bridge. A bridge that leads us closer to the heart of Christianity — a heart that beats with love, grace, and an unyielding hope for humanity. It's in these spaces of open dialogue and shared vulnerability that true understanding flourishes, and our world becomes a little more united, a little more divine.

Let's embrace these opportunities for exploration and explanation with openness and grace. In doing so, we not only dispel misconceptions but illuminate the path towards a more nuanced, compassionate, and comprehensive understanding of Christianity — a faith that, at its core, seeks to reconcile, renew, and inspire the world with the transformative power of love.

In the spirit of this journey, may every corrected misconception pave the way for deeper connections, richer dialogues, and a more inclusive understanding of the diverse and dynamic body of Christ. Together, let's celebrate the vast landscape of Christian thought, welcoming each question and challenge not as threats, but as invitations to deepen our faith and enrich our collective journey towards truth and understanding.

C. Practices and Exercises for Effective Apologetics

Embarking on the journey of effective apologetics, it's paramount to cultivate a foundation that's both robust and flexible. In a world teeming with questions, the ability to present Christianity in a clear, intelligent, and heartfelt manner is not just valuable but necessary. Herein lies a collection of practices and exercises designed to sharpen your skills in apologetics, fostering an environment where faith and reason coalesce harmoniously.

First, it's essential to understand that apologetics is not about winning arguments but rather about winning hearts. Start by practicing active listening. Engaging in conversations about faith, listen more than you speak. By truly understanding the questions and concerns of others, you can tailor your responses to address the core of their skepticism or curiosity.

Anchoring oneself in prayer is another fundamental practice. Prayer deepens your relationship with God and fortifies your spirit for the challenges that lie ahead. Before and after engaging in discussions about your faith, spend time in prayer, seeking guidance, wisdom, and patience. Remember, the journey of apologetics is as much inward as it is outward.

Diving into Scripture is invaluable. However, beyond mere reading, practice meditative reflection on key passages. Delve into the Gospels, the Acts of the Apostles, and the Letters, immersing yourself in the life and teachings of Jesus as well as the early Christians. This deep dive will not only solidify your understanding but also kindle a more profound love and passion for the message you're sharing.

Engage with both classic and contemporary Christian apologetics literature. By studying the works of great apologists across the ages, you'll gain a multifaceted perspective on how to articulate the tenets of Christianity effectively. Note their methods, how they address objections, and the manner in which they share the beauty and rationality of faith. This practice will also assist in identifying and refining your unique voice within the sphere of apologetics.

Exercise your reasoning and critical thinking skills. Christians are called not to a blind faith, but to a faith that seeks understanding. Engage in exercises that challenge you to think deeply about theological and philosophical questions. Use logic and reason to explore and explain the principles of your faith. This could be as simple as journaling your thoughts on tough questions or as engaging as participating in debates or discussions in study groups or online forums.

The art of storytelling cannot be underestimated. Practice narrating your personal journey with God and how your faith has transformed your life. Authentic, personal stories resonate deeply and can bridge gaps logical arguments cannot. By honing this skill, you become more adept at illustrating the impact of Christianity in a relatable, compelling manner.

Empathy is another crucial skill. Learn to position yourself in the shoes of skeptics and seekers, understanding their background, perspectives, and objections. Doing so not only equips you to address their concerns more effectively but also fosters an environment of respect and open dialogue.

Develop a habit of staying informed. In our rapidly changing world, being conversant with current events, scientific discoveries, and cultural trends is crucial. It empowers you to engage in relevant conversations, demonstrating how Christianity intersects with and speaks into the modern world.

Feedback is a gift. Seek it regularly from mentors, peers, and even skeptics. Engage in reflective practice, where you contemplate the feedback received to identify areas of strength and opportunities for growth. This iterative cycle of feedback and reflection fosters continuous improvement.

Empirical research is an often overlooked aspect of apologetics practice. Engage in studies or surveys that explore religious beliefs, behaviors, and the reasons behind faith transitions. This knowledge not only informs your apologetics but also deepens your empathy and understanding of the diverse landscape of belief and unbelief.

Participate in interfaith dialogue. Understanding other religious paradigms broadens your perspective, enriches your appreciation for the unique claims of Christianity, and sharpens your ability to communicate effectively in a pluralistic society.

Lastly, practice patience and perseverance. The journey of apologetics is marked by both breakthroughs and setbacks. Patience with yourself, with others, and with the process is essential. Persevere in love, knowing that each conversation is a seed planted, which, in time, may flourish in ways unseen.

Remember, effective apologetics is born out of a life deeply rooted in Christ. It flows naturally from a heart that knows and loves God intimately. By integrating these practices and exercises into your daily walk with Christ, you'll find yourself not only more equipped to engage in apologetics but also more deeply transformed by the very truths you seek to share.

As you embark on this journey, know that you are part of a rich tradition of believers who have navigated the challenges of their times with grace, wisdom, and courage. May you, too, rise to the call of presenting and living out the timeless truth of Christianity with clarity, compassion, and conviction.

Online Review Request for This Book

If this book has ignited a new understanding or reinforced your faith, sharing your perspective through an online review can enlighten others on their journey and extend the circle of this meaningful dialogue.

Printed in Great Britain
by Amazon

55643892R00071